To Troy - Thanks for Playing in
the recital. I hope this book can
be used of the Lord to enhance
your spiritual growth. II Tim. 2:1

Two Books In One

"No amount of money, genius, or culture can move things for God. Holiness energizing the soul, the whole man aflame with love, with desire for more faith, more prayer, more zeal, more consecration — this is the secret of power."

God is looking for individuals who will pray. **POWER THROUGH PRAYER** and **PURPOSE IN PRAYER** give the secrets of an effective prayer life and how to get results from God. The author gives examples of great men as well as the Apostles who made prayer a top priority in their lives and work. The challenge is for every Christian to make prayer a daily practice so that God can use each one effectively.

E. M. Bounds (1835-1913) practiced law for three years until he was called to preach, holding pastorates in Tennessee, Alabama and Missouri. He was editor of the *St. Louis Advocate,* and the *Christian Advocate.* In his busy life he daily scheduled the hours from four to seven in the morning for prayer.

Your prayer life will be enriched by reading these two Christian classics.

THE CHRISTIAN LIBRARY has been designed and produced for the discerning book lover. These classics of the Christian faith have been printed and bound with beauty, readability and longevity in mind.

Titles available include:

ABSOLUTE SURRENDER, Andrew Murray
BEN-HUR: A TALE OF THE CHRIST, Lew Wallace
THE CONFESSIONS OF ST. AUGUSTINE
THE GOD OF ALL COMFORT,
Hannah Whitall Smith
THE IMITATION OF CHRIST, Thomas a Kempis
IN HIS STEPS, Charles M. Sheldon
THE PILGRIMS PROGRESS, John Bunyan
POWER THROUGH PRAYER/
PURPOSE IN PRAYER, E.M. Bounds
QUIET TALKS ON PRAYER, S.D. Gordon

POWER THROUGH PRAYER
—
PURPOSE IN PRAYER

E.M. Bounds

Two Books In One

THE CHRISTIAN LIBRARY

ISBN 0-916441-03-2

(Canadian ISBN 0-919649-83-1)

Published by: THE CHRISTIAN LIBRARY
164 Mill Street
Westwood, New Jersey 07675

(In Canada, 960 The Gateway, Burlington, Ontario L7L 5K7)

EVANGELICAL CHRISTIAN PUBLISHERS ASSOCIATION ECPA MEMBER

Printed in the United States of America

POWER
THROUGH
PRAYER

1 Men of Prayer Needed

Study universal holiness of life. Your whole usefulness depends on this, for your sermons last but an hour or two; your life preaches all the week. If Satan can only make a covetous minister a lover of praise, of pleasure, of good eating, he has ruined your ministry. Give yourself to prayer, and get your texts, your thoughts, your words from God. Luther spent his best three hours in prayer. —Robert Murray McCheyne

We are constantly on a stretch, if not on a strain, to devise new methods, new plans, new organizations to advance the Church and secure enlargement and efficiency for the gospel. This trend of the day has a tendency to lose sight of the man or sink the man in the plan or organization. God's plan is to make much of the man, far more of him than of anything else. Men are God's method. The Church is looking for better methods; God is looking for better men. "There was a man sent from God whose name was John." The dispensation that heralded and prepared the way for Christ was bound up in that man John. "Unto us a child is born, unto us a son is given." The world's salvation comes out of that cradled Son. When Paul appeals to the personal character of the men who rooted the gospel in the world, he solves the mystery of their success. The glory and efficiency of the gospel is staked on the men who proclaim it. When God declares that "the eyes of the Lord run to and fro throughout the whole earth, to show himself strong in the behalf of them whose heart is perfect toward him," he declares the necessity of men and his dependence on them as a channel through which to exert his power upon the world. This vital, urgent truth is one that this age of machinery is apt to forget. The forgetting of it is as baneful on the work of God as would be the striking of the sun from his sphere. Darkness, confusion, and death would ensue.

What the Church needs today is not more machinery or better, not new organizations or more and novel methods, but men whom the Holy Ghost can use — men of prayer, men mighty in prayer. The Holy Ghost does not flow through methods, but through men. He does not come on machinery, but on men. He does not anoint plans, but men — men of prayer.

An eminent historian has said that the accidents of personal character have more to do with the revolutions of nations than either philosophic historians or democratic politicians will allow. This truth has its application in full to the gospel of Christ, the character and conduct of the followers of Christ — Christianize the world, transfigure nations and individuals. Of the preachers of the the gospel it is eminently true.

The character as well as the fortunes of the gospel is

committed to the preacher. He makes or mars the message from God to man. The preacher is the golden pipe through which the divine oil flows. The pipe must not only be golden, but open and flawless, that the oil may have a full, unhindered, unwasted flow.

The man makes the preacher. God must make the man. The messenger is, if possible, more than the message. The preacher is more than the sermon. The preacher makes the sermon. As the life-giving milk from the mother's bosom is but the mother's life, so all the preacher says is tinctured, impregnated by what the preacher is. The treasure is in earthen vessels, and the taste of the vessel impregnates and may discolor. The man, the whole man lies behind the sermon. Preaching is not the performance of an hour. It is the outflow of a life. It takes twenty years to make a sermon, because it takes twenty years to make the man. The true sermon is a thing of life. The sermon grows because the man grows. The sermon is forceful because the man is forceful. The sermon is holy because the man is holy. The sermon is full of the divine unction because the man is full of the divine unction.

Paul termed it "My gospel;" not that he had degraded it by his personal eccentricities or diverted it by selfish appropriation, but the gospel was put into the heart and lifeblood of the man Paul, as a personal trust to be executed by his Pauline traits, to be set aflame and empowered by the fiery energy of his fiery soul. Paul's sermons — what were they? Where are they? Skeletons, scattered fragments, afloat on the sea of inspiration! But the man Paul, greater than his sermons, lives forever, in full form, feature and stature, with his molding hand on the Church. The preaching is but a voice. The voice in silence dies, the text is forgotten, the sermon fades from memory; the preacher lives.

The sermon cannot rise in its life-giving forces above the man. Dead men give out dead sermons, and dead sermons kill. Everything depends on the spiritual character of the preacher. Under the Jewish dispensation the high priest had inscribed in jeweled letters on a golden frontlet: "Holiness to the Lord." So every preacher in Christ's ministry must be molded into and mastered by this same holy motto. It is a crying shame for the Christian ministry to fall lower in holiness of character and holiness of aim than the Jewish priesthood. Jonathan Edwards said: "I went on with my eager pursuit after more holiness and conformity to Christ. The heaven I desired was a heaven of holiness." The gospel of Christ does not move by popular waves. It has no self-propagating power. It moves as the men who have charge of it move. The preacher must impersonate the gospel. Its divine, most distinctive features must be embodied in him. The constraining power of love must be in the preacher as a projecting, eccentric, an all-commanding, self-oblivious force. The energy of self-denial must be his being, his heart and blood and bones. He must go forth as a man among men, clothed with humility, abiding in meekness, wise as a serpent, harmless as a dove; the bonds of a servant with the spirit of a king, a king in high, royal, independent bearing, with the simplicity and sweetness of a child. The preacher must throw himself, with all the abandon of a perfect, self-emptying faith and a self-consuming zeal, into his work for the salvation of men. Hearty, heroic, compassionate, fearless martyrs must the men be who take hold of and shape a generation for God. If they be timid timeservers, place seekers, if they be men pleasers or men fearers, if their faith has a weak hold on God or his Word, if their denial be broken by any phase of self or the world, they cannot take hold of the Church nor the world for God.

The preacher's sharpest and strongest preaching should be to himself. His most difficult, delicate, laborious, and thorough work must be with himself. The training of the twelve was the great, difficult, and enduring work of Christ. Preachers are not sermon makers, but men makers and saint makers, and he only is well-trained for this business who has made himself a man and a saint. It is not great talents nor great learning nor great preachers that God needs, but men great in holiness, great in faith, great in love, great in fidelity, great for God — men always preaching by holy sermons in the pulpit, by holy lives out of it. These can mold a generation for God.

After this order, the early Christians were formed. Men they were of solid mold, preachers after the heavenly type — heroic, stalwart, soldierly, saintly. Preaching with them meant self-denying, self-crucifying, serious, toilsome, martyr business. They applied themselves to it in a way that told on their generation, and formed in its womb a generation yet unborn for God. The preaching man is to be the praying man. Prayer is the preacher's mightiest weapon. An almighty force in itself, it gives life and force to all.

The real sermon is made in the closet. The man — God's man — is made in the closet. His life and his profoundest convictions were born in his secret communion with God. The burdened and tearful agony of his spirit, his weightiest and sweetest messages were got when alone with God. Prayer makes the man; prayer makes the preacher; prayer makes the pastor.

The pulpit of this day is weak in praying. The pride of learning is against the dependent humility of prayer. Prayer is with the pulpit too often only official — a performance for the routine of service. Prayer is not to the modern pulpit the mighty force it was in Paul's life or Paul's ministry. Every preacher who does not make prayer a mighty factor in his own life and ministry is weak as a factor in God's work and is powerless to project God's cause in this world.

2 Our Sufficiency Is of God

But above all he excelled in prayer. The inward-
ness and weight of his spirit, the reverence and solem-
nity of his address and behavior, and the fewness and
fullness of his words have often struck even strangers
with admiration as they used to reach others with con-
solation. The most awful, living, reverend frame I ever
felt or beheld, I must say, was his prayer. And truly it
was a testimony. He knew and lived nearer to the Lord
than other men, for they that know him most will see
most reason to approach him with reverence and fear.
—William Penn of George Fox

The sweetest graces by a slight perversion may bear
the bitterest fruit. The sun gives life, but sunstrokes are
death. Preaching is to give life; it may kill. The preacher
holds the keys; he may lock as well as unlock. Preaching

is God's great institution for the planting and maturing of spiritual life. When properly executed, its benefits are untold; when wrongly executed, no evil can exceed its damaging results. It is an easy matter to destroy the flock if the shepherd be unwary or the pasture be destroyed, easy to capture the citadel if the watchmen be asleep or the food and water be poisoned. Invested with such gracious prerogatives, exposed to so great evils, involving so many grave responsibilities, it would be a parody on the shrewdness of the devil and a libel on his character and reputation if he did not bring his master influences to adulterate the preacher and the preaching. In face of all this, the exclamatory interrogatory of Paul, "Who is sufficient for these things?" is never out of order.

Paul says: "Our sufficiency is of God, who also hath made us able ministers of the new testament; not of the letter, but of the spirit; for the letter killeth, but the spirit giveth life." The true ministry is God-touched, God-enabled, and God-made. The Spirit of God is on the preacher in anointing power, the fruit of the Spirit is in his heart, the Spirit of God has vitalized the man and the word; his preaching gives life, gives life as the spring gives life; gives life as the resurrection gives life; gives ardent life as the summer gives ardent life; gives fruitful life as the autumn gives fruitful life. The life-giving preacher is a man of God, whose heart is ever athirst for God, whose soul is ever following hard after God, whose eye is single to God, and in whom by the power of God's Spirit the flesh and the world have been crucified and his ministry is like the generous flood of a life-giving river.

The preaching that kills is nonspiritual preaching. The ability of the preaching is not from God. Lower sources than God have given to it energy and stimulant. The Spirit is not evident in the preacher nor his preaching. Many kinds of forces may be projected and stimulated by preaching that kills, but they are not spiritual forces. They may resemble spiritual forces, but are only the shadow, the counterfeit; life they may seem to have, but the life is magnetized. The preaching that kills is the letter; shapely and orderly it may be, but it is the letter still, the dry, husky, letter, the empty, bald shell. The letter may have the germ of life in it, but it has no breath of spring to evoke it; winter seeds they are, as hard as the winter's soil, as icy as the winter's air, no thawing nor germinating by them. This letter-preaching has the truth. But even divine truth has no life-giving energy alone; it must be energized by the Spirit, with all God's forces at its back. Truth unquickened by God's Spirit deadens as much as, or more than, error. It may be the truth without admixture; but without the Spirit its shade and touch are deadly, its truth error, its light darkness. The letter-preaching is unctionless, neither mellowed nor oiled by the Spirit. There may be tears, but tears cannot run God's machinery; tears may be but summer's breath on a snow-covered iceberg, nothing but surface slush. Feelings and earnestness there may be, but it is the emotion of the actor and the earnestness of the attorney. The preacher may feel from the kindling of his own sparks, be eloquent over his own exegesis, earnest in delivering the product of his own brain; the professor may usurp the place and imitate the fire of the apostle; brains and nerves may serve the place and feign the work of God's Spirit, and by these forces the letter may glow and sparkle like an illumined text, but the glow and sparkle will be as barren of life as the field sown with pearls. The death-dealing element lies back of the words, back of the sermon, back of the occasion, back of the manner, back of the action. The great hindrance is in the preacher himself. He has not in himself the mighty life-creating forces. There may be no discount on his orthodoxy, honesty, cleanliness, or earnestness; but somehow the man, the inner man, in his secret places has never broken down and surrendered to God, his inner life is not a great highway for the transmission of God's message, God's power. Somehow self and not God rules in the holy of holies. Somewhere, all unconscious to himself, some spiritual nonconductor has touched his inner being, and the divine current has been arrested. His inner being has never felt its thorough spiritual bankruptcy, its utter powerlessness; he has never learned to cry out with an ineffable cry of self-despair and self-helplessness till God's power and God's fire comes in and fills, purifies, empowers. Self-esteem, self-ability in some pernicious shape has defamed and violated the temple which should be held sacred for God. Life-giving preaching costs the preacher much — death to self, crucifixion to the world, the travail of his own soul. Crucified preaching can come only from a crucified man.

3 The Letter Killeth

During this affliction I was brought to examine my life in relation to eternity closer than I had done when in the enjoyment of health. In this examination relative to the discharge of my duties toward my fellow creatures as a man, a Christian minister, and an officer of the Church, I stood approved by my own conscience; but in relation to my Redeemer and Saviour the result was different. My returns of gratitude and loving obedience bear no proportion to my obligations for redeeming, preserving, and supporting me through the vicissitudes of life from infancy to old age. The coldness of my love to Him who first loved me and has done so much for me overwhelmed and confused me; and to complete my unworthy character, I had not only neglected to improve the grace given to the extent of my duty and privilege; but for want of improvement had, while abounding in perplexing care and labor, declined

from first zeal and love. I was confounded, humbled myself, implored mercy, and renewed by covenant to strive and devote myself unreservedly to the Lord.
—Bishop McKendree

The preaching that kills may be, and often is, orthodox — dogmatically, inviolably orthodox. We love orthodoxy. It is good. It is the best. It is the clean, clearcut teaching of God's Word, the trophies won by truth in its conflict with error, the levees which faith has raised against the desolating floods of honest or reckless misbelief or unbelief; but orthodoxy, clear and hard as crystal, suspicious and militant, may be but the letter well-shaped, well-named, and well-learned, the letter which kills. Nothing is so dead as a dead orthodoxy, too dead to speculate, too dead to think, to study, or to pray.

The preaching that kills may have insight and grasp of principles, may be scholarly and critical in taste, may have every minutiae of the derivation and grammar of the letter, may be able to trim the letter into its perfect pattern, and illume it as Plato and Cicero may be illumined, may study it as a lawyer studies his text-books to form his brief or to defend his case, and yet be like a frost, a killing frost. Letter-preaching may be eloquent, enameled with poetry and rhetoric, sprinkled with prayer, spiced with sensation, illumined by genius, and yet these be but the massive or chaste, costly mountings, the rare and beautiful flowers which coffin the corpse. The preaching which kills may be without scholarship, unmarked by any freshness of thought or feeling, clothed in tasteless generalities or vapid specialties, with style irregular, slovenly, savoring neither of closet nor of study, graced neither by thought, expression, or prayer. Under such preaching how wide and utter the desolation! how profound the spiritual death!

This letter-preaching deals with the surface and shadow of things, and not the things themselves. It does not penetrate the inner part. It has no deep insight into, nor strong grasp of, the hidden life of God's Word. It is true to the outside, but the outside is the hull which must be broken and penetrated for the kernel. The letter may be dressed so as to attract and be fashionable, but the attraction is not toward God nor is the fashion for heaven. The failure is in the preacher. God has not made him. He has never been in the hands of God like clay in the hands of the potter. He has been busy about the sermon, its thought and finish, its drawing and impressive forces; but the deep things of God have never been sought, studied, fathomed, experienced by him. He has never stood before "the throne high and lifted up," never heard the seraphim song, never seen the vision nor felt the rush of that awful holiness, and cried out in utter abandon and despair under the sense of weakness and guilt, and had his life renewed, his heart touched, purged, inflamed by the live coal from God's altar. His ministry may draw people to him, to the Church, to the form and ceremony; but no true drawings to God, no sweet, holy, divine communion induced. The Church has been frescoed but not edified, pleased but not sanctified. Life is suppressed; a chill is on the summer air; the soil is baked. The city of our God becomes the city of the dead; the Church a graveyard, not an embattled army. Praise and prayer are stifled; worship is dead. The preacher and the preaching have helped sin, not holiness; peopled hell, not heaven.

Preaching which kills is prayerless preaching. Without prayer the preacher creates death, and not life. The preacher who is feeble in prayer is feeble in life-giving power. Professional praying there is and will be, but professional praying helps the preaching to its deadly work. Professional praying chills and kills both preaching and praying. Much of the lax devotion and lazy irreverent attitudes in congregational praying are attributable to professional praying in the pulpit. Long, discursive, dry, and inane are the prayers in many pulpits. Without unction or heart, they fall like a killing frost on all the graces of worship. Death-dealing prayers they are. Every vestige of devotion has perished under their breath. The deader they are the longer they grow. A plea for short praying, live praying, real heart praying, praying by the Holy Spirit — direct, specific, ardent, simple, unctuous in the pulpit — is in order. A school to teach preachers how to pray, as God counts praying, would be more beneficial to true piety, true worship, and true preaching than all theological schools.

Stop! Pause! Consider! Where are we? What are we doing? Preaching to kill? Praying to kill? Praying to God! The great God, the Maker of all worlds, the Judge of all men! What reverence! What simplicity! What sincerity! What truth in the inward parts is demanded! How real we must be! How hearty! Prayer to God the noblest exercise, the loftiest effort of man, the most real thing! Shall we not discard forever accursed preaching that kills and prayer that kills, and do the real thing, the mightiest thing — prayerful praying, life-creating preaching, bring the mightiest force to bear on heaven and earth and draw on God's exhaustless and open treasure for the need and beggary of man?

4 Tendencies to Be Avoided

Let us often look at Brainerd in the woods of America pouring out his very soul before God for the perishing heathen without whose salvation nothing could make him happy. Prayer — secret, fervent, believing prayer — lies at the root of all personal godliness. A competent knowledge of the language where a missionary lives, a mild and winning temper, a heart given up to God in closet religion — these, these are the attainments which, more than all knowledge, or all other gifts, will fit us to become the instruments of God in the great work of human redemption.
                            —Carrey's Brotherhood, Serampore

There are two extreme tendencies in the ministry. The one is to shut itself out from intercourse with the people. The monk, the hermit were illustrations of this;

they shut themselves out from men to be more with God. They failed, of course. Our being with God is of use only as we expend its priceless benefits on men. This age, neither with preacher nor with people, is much intent on God. Our hankering is not that way. We shut ourselves to our study, we become students, bookworms, Bible worms, sermon makers, noted for literature, thought, and sermons; but the people and God, where are they? Out of heart, out of mind. Preachers who are great thinkers, great students must be the greatest of prayers, or else they will be the greatest of backsliders, heartless professionals, rationalistic, less than the least of preachers in God's estimate.

The other tendency is to thoroughly popularize the ministry. He is no longer God's man, but a man of affairs, of the people. He prays not, because his mission is to the people. If he can move the people, create an interest, a sensation in favor of religion, an interest in Church work — he is satisfied. His personal relation to God is no factor in his work. Prayer has little or no place in his plans. The disaster and ruin of such a ministry cannot be computed by earthly arithmetic. What the preacher is in prayer to God, for himself, for his people, so is his power for real good to men, so is his true fruitfulness, his true fidelity to God, to man, for time, for eternity.

It is impossible for the preacher to keep his spirit in harmony with the divine nature of his high calling without much prayer. That the preacher by dint of duty and laborious fidelity to the work and routine of the ministry can keep himself in trim and fitness is a serious mistake. Even sermon-making, incessant and taxing as an art, as a duty, as a work, or as a pleasure, will engross and harden, will estrange the heart, by neglect of prayer, from God. The scientist loses God in nature. The preacher may lose God in his sermon.

Prayer freshens the heart of the preacher, keeps it in tune with God and in sympathy with the people, lifts his ministry out of the chilly air of a profession, fructifies routine and moves every wheel with the facility and power of a divine unction.

Mr. Spurgeon says: "Of course the preacher is above all others distinguished as a man of prayer. He prays as an ordinary Christian, else he were a hypocrite. He prays more than ordinary Christians, else he were disqualified for the office he has undertaken. If you as ministers are not very prayerful, you are to be pitied. If you become lax in sacred devotion, not only will you need to be pitied but your people also, and the day cometh in which you shall be ashamed and confounded. All our libraries and studies are mere emptiness compared with our closets. Our seasons of fasting and prayer at the Tabernacle have been high days indeed; never have our hearts been nearer the central Glory."

The praying which makes a prayerful ministry is not a little praying put in as we put flavor to give it a pleasant smack, but the praying must be in the body, and form the blood and bones. Prayer is no petty duty, put into a corner; no piecemeal performance made out of the fragments of time which have been snatched from business and other engagements of life; but it means that the best of our time, the heart of our time and strength must be given. It does not mean the closet absorbed in the study or swallowed up in the activities of ministerial duties; but it means the closet first, the study and activities second, both study and activities freshened and made efficient by the closet. Prayer that affects one's ministry must give tone to one's life. The praying which gives color and bent to character is no pleasant, hurried pastime. It must enter as strongly into the heart and life as Christ's "strong crying and tears" did; must draw out the soul into an agony of desire as Paul's did; must be an inwrought fire and force like the "effectual, fervent prayer" of James; must be of that quality which, when put into the golden censer and incensed before God, works mighty spiritual throes and revolutions.

Prayer is not a little habit pinned on to us while we were tied to our mother's apron strings; neither is it a little decent quarter of a minute's grace said over an hour's dinner, but it is a most serious work of our most serious years. It engages more of time and appetite than our longest dinings or richest feasts. The prayer that makes much of our preaching must be made much of. The character of our praying will determine the character of our preaching. Light praying will make light preaching. Prayer makes preaching strong, gives it unction, and makes it stick. In every ministry weighty for good, prayer has always been a serious business.

The preacher must be preeminently a man of prayer. His heart must graduate in the school of prayer. In the school of prayer only can the heart learn to preach. No learning can make up for the failure to pray. No earnestness, no diligence, no study, no gifts will supply its lack.

Talking to men for God is a great thing, but talking to God for men is greater still. He will never talk well and with real success to men for God who has not learned well how to talk to God for men. More than this, prayerless words in the pulpit and out of it are deadening words.

5 Prayer, the Great Essential

You know the value of prayer: it is precious beyond all price. Never, never neglect it.
— Sir Thomas Buxton

Prayer is the first thing, the second thing, the third thing necessary to a minister. Pray, then, my dear brother; pray, pray, pray. — Edward Payson

Prayer, in the preacher's life, in the preacher's study, in the preacher's pulpit, must be a conspicuous and an all-impregnating force and an all-coloring ingredient. It must play no secondary part, be no mere coating. To him it is given to be with his Lord "all night in prayer." The preacher, to train himself in self-denying prayer, is charged look to his Master, who, "rising up a great while before day, went out, and departed into a solitary place, and there prayed." The preacher's study ought to be a closet, a Bethel, an altar, a vision, and a ladder, that every thought might ascend heavenward ere it went manward; that every part of the sermon might be scented by the air of heaven and made serious, because God was in the study.

As the engine never moves until the fire is kindled, so preaching, with all its machinery, perfection, and polish, is at a dead standstill, as far as spiritual results are concerned, till prayer has kindled and created the steam. The texture, fineness, and strength of the sermon is as so much rubbish unless the mighty impulse of prayer is in it, through it, and behind it. The preacher must, by prayer, put God in the sermon. The preacher must, by prayer, move God toward the people before he can move the people to God by his words. The preacher must have had audience and ready access to God before he can have access to the people. An open way to God for the preacher is the surest pledge of an open way to the people.

It is necessary to iterate and reiterate that prayer, as a mere habit, as a performance gone through by routine or in a professional way, is a dead and rotten thing. Such praying has no connection with the praying for which we plead. We are stressing true praying, which engages and sets on fire every high element of the preacher's being — prayer which is born of vital oneness with Christ and the fullness of the Holy Ghost, which springs from the deep, overflowing fountains of tender compassion, deathless solicitude for man's eternal good; a consuming zeal for the glory of God; a thorough conviction of the preacher's difficult and delicate work and of the imperative need of God's mightiest help. Praying grounded on these solemn and profound convictions is the only true praying. Preaching backed by such praying is the only preaching which sows the seeds of eternal life in human hearts and builds men up for heaven.

It is true that there may be popular preaching, pleasant preaching, taking preaching, preaching of much intellectual, literary, and brainy force, with its measure and form of good, with little or no praying; but the preaching which secures God's end in preaching must be born of prayer from text to exordium, delivered with the energy and spirit of prayer, followed and made to germinate, and kept in vital force in the hearts of the hearers by the preacher's prayers, long after the occasion has passed.

We may excuse the spiritual poverty of our preaching in many ways, but the true secret will be found in the lack of urgent prayer for God's presence in the power of the Holy Spirit. There are preachers innumerable who can deliver masterful sermons after their order; but the effects are short-lived and do not enter as a factor at all into the regions of the spirit where the fearful war between God and Satan, heaven and hell, is being waged because they are not made powerfully militant and spiritually victorious by prayer.

The preachers who gain mighty results for God are the men who have prevailed in their pleadings with God ere venturing to plead with men. The preachers who are the mightiest in their closets with God are the mightiest in their pulpits with men.

Preachers are human folks, and are exposed to and often caught by the strong driftings of human currents. Praying is spiritual work; and human nature does not like taxing, spiritual work. Human nature wants to sail to heaven under a favoring breeze, a full, smooth sea. Prayer is humbling work. It abases intellect and price, crucifies vainglory, and signs our spiritual bankruptcy, and all these are hard for flesh and blood to bear. It is easier not to pray than to bear them. So we come to one

of the crying evils of these times, maybe of all times —
little or no praying. Of these two evils, perhaps little
praying is worse than no praying. Little praying is a
kind of make-believe, a salve for the conscience, a farce
and a delusion.

The little estimate we put on prayer is evident from
the little time we give to it. The time given to prayer by
the average preacher scarcely counts in the sum of the
daily aggregate. Not infrequently the preacher's only
praying is by his bedside in his nightdress, ready for bed
and soon in it, with, perchance, the addition of a few
hasty snatches of prayer ere he is dressed in the morning. How feeble, vain, and little is such praying compared with the time and energy devoted to praying by
holy men in and out of the Bible! How poor and mean
our petty, childish praying is beside the habits of the
true men of God in all ages! To men who think praying
their main business and devote time to it according to
this high estimate of its importance does God commit
the keys of his kingdom, and by them does he work his
spiritual wonders in this world. Great praying is the sign
and seal of God's great leaders and the earnest of the
conquering forces with which God will crown their
labors.

The preacher is commissioned to pray as well as to
preach. His mission is incomplete if he does not do both
well. The preacher may speak with all the eloquence of
men and of angels; but unless he can pray with a faith
which draws all heaven to his aid, his preaching will be
"as sounding brass or a tinkling cymbal" for permanent
God-honoring, soul-saving uses.

6 A Praying Ministry Successful

The principal cause of my leanness and unfruitfulness is owing to an unaccountable backwardness to pray. I can write or read or converse or hear with a ready heart; but prayer is more spiritual and inward than any of these, and the more spiritual any duty is the more my carnal heart is apt to start from it. Prayer and patience and faith are never disappointed. I have long since learned that if ever I was to be a minister faith and prayer must make me one. When I can find my heart in frame and liberty for prayer, everything else is comparatively easy. —Richard Newton

It may be put down as a spiritual axiom that in every truly successful ministry prayer is an evident and controlling force — evident and controlling in the life of the preacher, evident and controlling in the deep spirituality of his work. A ministry may be a very thoughtful ministry without prayer; the preacher may secure fame and popularity without prayer; the whole machinery of the preacher's life and work may be run without the oil of prayer or with scarcely enough to grease one cog; but no ministry can be a spiritual one, securing holiness in the preacher and in his people, without prayer being made an evident and controlling force.

The preacher that prays indeed puts God into the work. God does not come into the preacher's work as a matter of course or on general principles, but he comes by prayer and special urgency. That God will be found of us in the day that we seek him with the whole heart is as true of the preacher as of the penitent. A prayerful ministry is the only ministry that brings the preacher into sympathy with the people. Prayer as essentially unites to the human as it does to the divine. A prayerful ministry is the only ministry qualified for the high offices and responsibilities of the preacher. Colleges, learning, books, theology, preaching, cannot make a preacher, but praying does. The apostles' commission to preach was a blank till filled up by the Pentecost which praying brought. A prayerful minister has passed beyond the regions of the popular, beyond the man of mere affairs, of secularities, of pulpit attractiveness; passed beyond the ecclesiastical organizer or general into a sublimer and mightier region, the region of the spiritual. Holiness is the product of his work; transfigured hearts and lives emblazon the reality of his work, its trueness and substantial nature. God is with him. His ministry is not projected on worldly or surface principles. He is deeply stored with and deeply schooled in the things of God. His long, deep communings with God about his people and the agony of his wrestling spirit have crowned him as a prince in the things of God. The iciness of the mere professional has long since melted under the intensity of his praying.

The superficial results of many a ministry, the deadness of others, are to be found in the lack of praying. No ministry can succeed without much praying, and this praying must be fundamental, ever-abiding, ever-increasing. The text, the sermon, should be the result of prayer. The study should be bathed in prayer, all its duties impregnated with prayer, its whole spirit the spirit of prayer. "I am sorry that I have prayed so little," was the deathbed regret of one of God's chosen ones, a sad and remorseful regret for a preacher. "I want a life of greater, deeper, truer prayer," said the late Archbishop Tait. So may we all say, and this may we all secure.

God's true preachers have been distinguished by one great feature: they were men of prayer. Differing often in many things, they have always had a common center. They may have started from different points, and traveled by different roads, but they converged to one point: they were one in prayer. God to them was the center of attraction, and prayer was the path that led to God. These men prayed not occasionally, not a little at regular or at odd times; but they so prayed that their prayers entered into and shaped their characters; they so prayed as to affect their own lives and the lives of others; they so prayed as to make the history of the Church and influence the current of the times. They spent much time in prayer, not because they marked the shadow on the dial or the hands on the clock, but because it was to them so momentous and engaging a business that they could scarcely give over.

Prayer was to them what it was to Paul, a striving with earnest effort of soul; what it was to Jacob, a wrestling and prevailing; what it was to Christ, "strong crying and tears." They "prayed always with all prayer and supplication in the Spirit, and watching thereunto with

31

all perseverance." "The effectual, fervent prayer" has been the mightiest weapon of God's mightiest soldiers. The statement in regard to Elijah — that he "was a man subject to like passions as we are, and he prayed earnestly that it might not rain; and it rained not on the earth by the space of three years and six months. And he prayed again, and the heaven gave rain, and the earth brought forth her fruit" — comprehends all prophets and preachers who have moved their generation for God, and shows the instrument by which they worked their wonders.

7 Much Time Should Be Given to Prayer

The great masters and teachers in Christian doctrine have always found in prayer their highest source of illumination. Not to go beyond the limits of the English Church, it is recorded of Bishop Andrews that he spent five hours daily on his knees. The greatest practical resolves that have enriched and beautified human life in Christian times have been arrived at in prayer.
—Canon Liddon

While many private prayers, in the nature of things, must be short; while public prayers, as a rule, ought to be short and condensed; while there is ample room for and value put on ejaculatory prayer — yet in our private communications with God time is a feature essential to its value. Much time spent with God is the secret of all successful praying. Prayer which is felt as a mighty force is the mediate or immediate product of much time spent with God. Our short prayers owe their point and efficiency to the long ones that have preceded them. The short prevailing prayer cannot be prayed by one who has not prevailed with God in a mightier struggle of long continuance. Jacob's victory of faith could not have been gained without that all-night wrestling. God's acquaintance is not made by pop calls. God does not bestow his gifts on the casual or hasty comers and goers. Much with God alone is the secret of knowing him and of influence with him. He yields to the persistency of a faith that knows him. He bestows his richest gifts upon those who declare their desire for and appreciation of those gifts by the constancy as well as earnestness of their importunity. Christ, who in this as well as other things is our Example, spent many whole nights in prayer. His custom was to pray much. He had his habitual place to pray. Many long seasons of praying make up his history and character. Paul prayed day and night. It took time from very important interests for Daniel to pray three times a day. David's morning, noon, and night praying were doubtless on many occasions very protracted. While we have no specific account of the time these Bible saints spent in prayer, yet the indications are that they consumed much time in prayer, and on some occasions long seasons of praying was their custom.

We would not have any think that the value of their prayers is be measured by the clock, but our purpose is to impress on our minds the necessity of being much alone with God; and that if this feature has not been produced by our faith, then our faith is of a feeble and surface type.

The men who have most fully illustrated Christ in their character, and have most powerfully affected the world for him, have been men who spent so much time with God as to make it a notable feature of their lives. Charles Simeon devoted the hours from four till eight in the morning to God. Mr. Wesley spent two hours daily in prayer. He began at four in the morning. Of him, one who knew him well wrote: "He thought prayer to be more his business than anything else, and I have seen him come out of his closet with a serenity of face next to shining." John Fletcher stained the walls of his room by the breath of his prayers. Sometimes he would pray all night; always, frequently, and with great earnestness. His whole life was a life of prayer. "I would not rise from my seat," he said, "without lifting my heart to God." His greeting to a friend was always: "Do I meet you praying?" Luther said: "If I fail to spend two hours in prayer each morning, the devil gets the victory through the day. I have so much business I cannot get on without spending three hours daily in prayer." He had a motto: "He that has prayed well has studied well."

Archbishop Leighton was so much alone with God that he seemed to be in a perpetual meditation. "Prayer and praise were his business and his pleasure," says his biographer. Bishop Ken was so much with God that his soul was said to be God-enamored. He was with God before the clock struck three every morning. Bishop Asbury said: "I propose to rise at four o'clock as often as I can and spend two hours in prayer and meditation." Samuel Rutherford, the fragrance of whose piety is still rich, rose at three in the morning to meet God in prayer. Joseph Alleine arose at four o'clock for his business of praying till eight. If he heard other tradesmen plying their business before he was up, he would exclaim: "O how this shames me! Does not my Master deserve more than theirs?" He who has learned this trade well draws at will, on sight, and with acceptance of heaven's unfailing bank.

One of the holiest and among the most gifted of Scotch preachers says: "I ought to spend the best hours in communion with God. It is my noblest and most fruitful employment, and is not to be thrust into a corner. The morning hours, from six to eight, are the most uninterrupted and should be thus employed. After tea is my best hour, and that should be solemnly dedicated to God. I ought not to give up the good old habit of prayer before going to bed; but guard must be kept against sleep. When I awake in the night, I ought to rise and pray. A little time after breakfast might be given to intercession." This was the praying plan of Robert McCheyne. The memorable Methodist band in their praying shame us. "From four to five in the morning, private prayer; from five to six in the evening, private prayer."

John Welch, the holy and wonderful Scotch preacher, thought the day ill spent if he did not spend eight or ten hours in prayer. He kept a plaid that he might wrap himself when he arose to pray at night. His wife would complain when she found him lying on the ground weeping. He would reply: "O woman, I have the souls of three thousand to answer for, and I know not how it is with many of them!"

8 Examples of Praying Men

The act of praying is the very highest energy of which the human mind is capable; praying, that is, with the total concentration of the faculties. The great mass of worldly men and of learned men are absolutely incapable of prayer. —Samuel Taylor Coleridge

Bishop Wilson says: "In H. Martyn's journal the spirit of prayer, the time he devoted to the duty, and his fervor in it are the first things which strike me."

Payson wore the hard-wood boards into grooves where his knees pressed so often and so long. His biographer says: "His continuing instant in prayer, be his circumstances what they might, is the most noticeable fact in his history, and points out the duty of all who would rival his eminency. To his ardent and persevering prayers must no doubt be ascribed in a great measure his distinguished and almost uninterrupted success.''

The Marquis DeRenty, to whom Christ was most precious, ordered his servant to call him from his devotions at the end of half an hour. The servant at the time saw his face through an aperture. It was marked with such holiness that he hated to arouse him. His lips were moving, but he was perfectly silent. He waited until three half hours had passed; then he called to him, when he arouse from his knees, saying that the half hour was so short when he was communing with Christ.

Brainerd said: ''I love to be alone in my cottage, where I can spend much time in prayer.''

William Bramwell is famous in Methodist annals for personal holiness and for his wonderful success in preaching and for the marvelous answers to his prayers. For hours at a time he would pray. He almost lived on his knees. He went over his circuits like a flame of fire. The fire was kindled by the time he spent in prayer. He often spent as much as four hours in a single season of prayer in retirement.

Bishop Andrewes spent the greatest part of five hours every day in prayer and devotion.

Sir Henry Havelock always spent the first two hours of each day alone with God. If the encampment was struck at 6 a.m., he would rise at four.

Earl Cairns rose daily at six o'clock to secure an hour and a half for the study of the Bible and for prayer, before conducting family worship at a quarter to eight.

Dr. Judson's success in prayer is attributable to the fact that he gave much time to prayer. He says on this point: ''Arrange thy affairs, if possible, so that thou canst leisurely devote two or three hours every day not merely to devotional exercise but to the very act of secret prayer and communion with God. Endeavor seven times a day to withdraw from business and company and lift up thy soul to God in private retirement.

Begin the day by rising after midnight and devoting some time amid the silence and darkness of the night to this sacred work. Let the hour of opening dawn find thee at the same work. Let the hours nine, twelve, three, six, and nine at night witness the same. Be resolute in His cause. Make all practicable sacrifices to maintain it. Consider that thy time is short, and that business and company must not be allowed to rob thee of thy God." Impossible, say we, fanatical directions! Dr. Judson impressed an empire for Christ and laid the foundations of God's kingdom with imperishable granite in the heart of Burmah. He was successful, one of the few men who mightily impressed the world for Christ. Many men of greater gifts and genius and learning than he have made no such impression; their religious work is like footsteps in the sands, but he has engraven his work on the adamant. The secret of its profundity and endurance is found in the fact that he gave time to prayer. He kept the iron red-hot with prayer, and God's skill fashioned it with enduring power. No man can do a great and enduring work for God who is not a man of prayer, and no man can be a man of prayer who does not give much time to praying.

Is it true that prayer is simply the compliance with habit, dull and mechanical? A petty performance into which we are trained till tameness, shortness, superficiality are its chief elements? "Is it true that prayer is, as is assumed, little else than the half-passive play of sentiment which flows languidly on through the minutes or hours of easy reverie?" Canon Liddon continues: "Let those who have really prayed give the answer. They sometimes describe prayer with the patriarch Jacob as a wrestling together with an Unseen Power which may last, not infrequently in an earnest life, late into the night hours, or even to the break of day. Sometimes they refer to common intercession with St. Paul as a concerted struggle. They have, when praying, their eyes fixed on the Great Intercessor in Gethsemane, upon the drops of blood which fall to the ground in that agony of resignation and sacrifice. Importunity is of the essence of successful prayer. Importunity means not dreaminess but sustained work. It is through prayer especially that the kingdom of heaven suffereth violence and the violent take it by force. It was a saying of the late Bishop Hamilton that "No man is likely to do much good in prayer who does not begin by looking upon it in the light of a work to be prepared for and persevered in with all the earnestness which we bring to bear upon subjects which are in our opinion at once most interesting and most necessary."

9 Begin the Day with Prayer

I ought to pray before seeing anyone. Often when I sleep long, or meet with others early, it is eleven or twelve o'clock before I begin secret prayer. This is a wretched system. It is unscriptural. Christ arose before day and went into solitary place. David says: "Early will I seek thee; Thou shalt early hear my voice." Family prayer loses much of its power and sweetness, and I can do no good to those who come to seek from me. The conscience feels guilty, the soul unfed, the lamp not trimmed. Then when in secret prayer the soul is often out of tune. I feel it is far better to begin with God — to see his face first, to get my soul near him before it is near another. —Robert Murray McCheyne

The men who have done the most for God in this world have been early on their knees. He who fritters away the early morning, its opportunity and freshness, in other pursuits than seeking God will make poor headway seeking him the rest of the day. If God is not first in our thoughts and efforts in the morning, he will be in the last place the remainder of the day.

Behind this early rising and early praying is the ardent desire which presses us into this pursuit after God. Morning listlessness is the index to a listless heart. The heart which is behindhand in seeking God in the morning has lost its relish for God. David's heart was ardent after God, and so he sought God early, before daylight. The bed and sleep could not chain his soul in its eagerness after God. Christ longed for communion with God; and so, rising a great while before day, he would go out into the mountain to pray. The disciples, when fully awake and ashamed of their indulgence, would know where to find him. We might go through the list of men who have mightily impressed the world for God, and we would find them early after God.

A desire for God which cannot break the chains of sleep is a weak thing and will do but little good for God after it has indulged itself fully. The desire for God that keeps so far behind the devil and the world at the beginning of the day will never catch up.

It is not simply the getting up that puts men to the front and makes them captain generals in God's hosts, but it is the ardent desire which stirs and breaks all self-indulgent chains. But the getting up gives vent, increase, and strength to the desire. If they had lain in bed and indulged themselves, the desire would have been quenched. The desire aroused them and put them on the stretch for God, and this heeding and acting on the call gave their faith its grasp on God and gave to their hearts the sweetest and fullest revelation of God, and this strength of faith and fullness of revelation made them saints by eminence, and the halo of their sainthood has come down to us, and we have entered on the enjoyment of their conquests. But we take our fill in enjoyment, and not in productions. We build their tombs and write their epitaphs, but are careful not to follow their examples.

We need a generation of preachers who seek God and seek him early, who give the freshness and dew of effort to God, and secure in return the freshness and fullness of his power that he may be as the dew to them, full of gladness and strength, through all the heat and labor of the day. Our laziness after God is our crying sin. The children of this world are far wiser than we. They are at it early and late. We do not seek God with ardor and diligence. No man gets God who does not follow hard after him, and no soul follows hard after God who is not after him in early morn.

10 Prayer and Devotion United

There is a manifest want of spiritual influence on the ministry of the present day. I feel it in my own case and I see it in that of others. I am afraid there is too much of a low, managing, contriving, maneuvering temper of mind among us. We are laying ourselves out more than is expedient to meet one man's taste and another man's prejudices. The ministry is a grand and holy affair, and it should find in us a simple habit of spirit and a holy but humble indifference to all consequences. The leading defect in Christian ministers is want of a devotional habit. —Richard Cecil

Never was there a greater need for saintly men and women; more imperative still is the call for saintly, God-devoted preachers. The world moves with gigantic strides. Satan has his hold and rule on the world, and labors to make all its movements subserve his ends. Religion must do its best work, present its most attractive and perfect models. By every means, modern sainthood must be inspired by the loftiest ideals and by the largest possibilities through the Spirit. Paul lived on his knees, that the Ephesian Church might measure the heights, breadths, and depths of an unmeasurable saintliness, and "be filled with all the fullness of God." Epaphras laid himself out with the exhaustive toil and strenuous conflict of fervent prayer, that the Colossian Church might "stand perfect and complete in all the will of God." Everywhere, everything in apostolic times was on the stretch that the people of God might each and "all come in the unity of the faith, and of the knowledge of the Son of God, unto a perfect man, unto the measure of the stature of the fullness of Christ." No premium was given to dwarfs; no encouragement to an old babyhood. The babies were to grow; the old, instead of feebleness and infirmities, were to bear fruit in old age, and be fat and flourishing. The divinest thing in religion is holy men and holy women.

No amount of money, genius, or culture can move things for God. Holiness energizing the soul, the whole man aflame with love, with desire for more faith, more prayer, more zeal, more consecration — this is the secret of power. These we need and must have, and men must be the incarnation of this God-inflamed devotedness. God's advance has been stayed, his cause crippled, his name dishonored for their lack. Genius (though the loftiest and most gifted), education (though the most learned and refined), position, dignity, place, honored names, high ecclesiastics cannot move this chariot of our God. It is a fiery one, and fiery forces only can move it. The genius of a Milton fails. The imperial strength of a Leo fails. Brainerd's spirit can move it. Brainerd's spirit was on fire for God, on fire for souls.

Nothing earthly, worldly, selfish came in to abate in the least the intensity of this all-impelling and all-consuming force and flame.

Prayer is the creator as well as the channel of devotion. The spirit of devotion is the spirit of prayer. Prayer and devotion are united as soul and body are united, as life and heart are united. There is no real prayer without devotion, no devotion without prayer. The preacher must be surrendered to God in the holiest devotion. He is not a professional man, his ministry is not a profession; it is a divine institution, a divine devotion. He is devoted to God. His aim, aspirations, ambition are for God and to God, and to such prayer is as essential as food is to life.

The preacher, above everything else, must be devoted to God. The preacher's relations to God are the insignia and credentials of his ministry. These must be clear, conclusive, unmistakable. No common, surface type of piety must be his. If he does not excel in grace, he does not excel at all. If he does not preach by life, character, conduct, he does not preach at all. If his piety be light, his preaching may be as soft and as sweet as music, as gifted as Apollo, yet its weight will be a feather's weight, visionary, fleeting as the morning cloud or the early dew. Devotion to God — there is no substitute for this in the preacher's character and conduct. Devotion to a Church, to opinions, to an organization, to orthodoxy — these are paltry, misleading, and vain when they become the source of inspiration, the animus of a call. God must be the mainspring of the preacher's effort, the fountain and crown of all his toil. The name and honor of Jesus Christ, the advance of His cause, must be all in all. The preacher must have no inspiration but the name of Jesus Christ, no ambition but to have Him glorified, no toil but for Him. Then prayer will be a source of His illuminations, the means of perpetual advance, the gauge of his success. The perpetual aim, the only ambition, the preacher can cherish is to have God with him.

Never did the cause of God need perfect illustrations of the possibilities of prayer more than in this age. No age, no person, will be ensamples of the gospel power except the ages or persons of deep and earnest prayer. A prayerless age will have but scant models of divine power. Prayerless hearts will never rise to these Alpine heights. The age may be a better age than the past, but there is an infinite distance between the betterment of an age by the force of an advancing civilization and its betterment by the increase of holiness and Christlikeness by the energy of prayer. The Jews were much better when Christ came than in the ages before. It was the golden age of their Pharisaic religion. Their golden religious age crucified Christ. Never more praying, never less praying; never more sacrifices, never less sacrifice; never less idolatry, never more idolatry; never more of temple worship, never less of God worship; never more of lip service, never less of heart service (God worshiped by lips whose hearts and hands crucified God's Son!); never more of church-goers, never less of saints.

It is prayer-force which makes saints. Holy characters are formed by the power of real praying. The more of true saints, the more of praying; the more of praying, the more of true saints.

11 An Example of Devotion

I urge upon you communion with Christ, a growing communion. There are curtains to be drawn aside in Christ that we never saw, and new foldings of love in Him. I despair that I shall ever with to the far end of that love, there are so many plies in it. Therefore dig deep, and sweat and labor and take pains for Him, and set by as much time in the day for Him as you can. He will be won in the labor. —Samuel Rutherford

God has now, and has had, many of these devoted, prayerful preachers — men in whose lives prayer has been a mighty, controlling conspicuous force. The world has felt their power, God has felt and honored their power, God's cause has moved mightily and swiftly by their prayers, holiness has shone out in their characters with a divine effulgence.

God found one of the men he was looking for in David Brainerd, whose work and name have gone into history. He was no ordinary man, but was capable of shining in any company, the peer of the wise and gifted ones, eminently suited to fill the most attractive pulpits and to labor among the most refined and the cultured, who were so anxious to secure him for their pastor. President Edwards bears testimony that he was "a young man of distinguished talents, had extraordinary knowledge of men and things, had rare conversational powers, excelled in his knowledge of theology, and was truly, for one so young, an extraordinary divine, and especially in all matters relating to experimental religion. I never knew his equal of his age and standing for clear and accurate notions of the nature and essence of true religion. His manner in prayer was almost inimitable, such as I have very rarely known equaled. His learning was very considerable, and he had extraordinary gifts for the pulpit."

No sublimer story has been recorded in earthly annals than that of David Brainerd; no miracle attests with diviner force the truth of Christianity than the life and work of such a man. Alone in the savage wilds of America, struggling day and night with a mortal disease, unschooled in the care of souls, having access to the Indians for a large portion of time only through the bungling medium of a pagan interpreter, with the Word of God in his heart and in his hand, his soul fired with the divine flame, a place and time to pour out his soul to God in prayer, he fully established the worship of God and secured all its gracious results. The Indians were changed with a great change from the lowest besotments of an ignorant and debased heathenism to pure, devout, intelligent Christians; all vice reformed, the external duties of Christianity at once embraced and acted on; family prayer set up; the Sabbath instituted and religiously observed; the internal graces of religion exhibited with growing sweetness and strength. The solution of these results is found in David Brainerd himself, not in the conditions or accidents but in the man Brainerd. He was God's man, for God first and last and all the time. God could flow unhindered through him. The omnipotence of grace was neither arrested nor straightened by the conditions of his heart; the whole channel was broadened and cleaned out for God's fullest and most powerful passage, so that God with all his mighty forces could come down on the hopeless, savage wilderness, and transform it into his blooming and fruitful garden; for nothing is too hard for God to do if he can get the right kind of man to do it with.

Brainerd lived the life of holiness and prayer. His diary is full and monotonous with the record of his seasons of fasting, meditation, and retirement. The time he spent in private prayer amounted to many hours daily. "When I return home," he said, "and give myself to meditation, prayer, and fasting, my soul longs for mortification, self-denial, humility, and divorcement from all things of the world." "I have nothing to do," he said, "with earth, but only to labor in it honestly for God. I do not desire to live one minute for anything which earth can afford." After this high order did he pray: "Feeling somewhat of the sweetness of communion with God and the constraining force of his love, and how admirably it captivates the soul and makes all the desires and affections to center in God, I set apart this day for secret fasting and prayer, to entreat God to direct and bless me with regard to the great work which I have in view of preaching the gospel and that the Lord would return to me and show me the light of his countenance. I had little life and power in the forenoon. Near the middle of the afternoon God enabled me to wrestle ardently in intercession for my absent frineds, but just at night the Lord visited me marvelously in prayer. I think my soul was never in such agony before. I felt no restraint, for the treasures of divine grace were opened to me. I wrestled for absent friends, for the ingathering of souls, for multitudes of poor souls, and for many that I thought were the children of God, personally, in many distant places. I was in such agony from sun half an hour high till near dark that I was all over wet with sweat, but yet it seemed to me I had done nothing. O, my dear Saviour did sweat blood for poor souls! I longed for more compassion toward them. I felt still in a sweet frame, under a sense of divine love and grace, and went to bed in such a frame, with my heart set on God." It was prayer which gave to his life and ministry their marvelous power.

The men of mighty prayer are men of spiritual might. Prayers never die. Brainerd's whole life was a life of prayer. By day and by night he prayed. Before preaching and after preaching he prayed. Riding through the interminable solitudes of the forests he prayed. On his bed of straw he prayed. Retiring to the dense and lonely forests, he prayed. Hour by hour, day after day, early morn and late at night, he was praying and fasting, pouring out his soul, interceding, communing with God. He was with God mightily in prayer, and God was with him mightily, and by it he being dead yet speaketh and worketh, and will speak and work till the end comes, and among the glorious ones of that glorious day he will be with the first.

Jonathan Edwards says of him: "His life shows the right way to success in the works of the ministry. He sought it as the soldier seeks victory in a siege or battle; or as a man that runs a race for a great prize. Animated with love to Christ and souls, how did he labor? Always fervently. Not only in word and doctrine, in public and in private, but in prayers by day and night, wrestling with God in secret and travailing in birth with unutterable groans and agonies, until Christ was formed in the hearts of the people to whom he was sent. Like a true son of Jacob, he persevered in wrestling through all the darkness of the night, until the breaking of the day!"

12 Heart Preparation Necessary

For nothing reaches the heart but what is from the heart, or pierces the conscience but what comes from a living conscience. —William Penn

In the morning was more engaged in preparing the head than the heart. This has been frequently my error, and I have always felt the evil of it, especially in prayer. Reform it, then, O Lord! Enlarge my heart, and I shall preach. —Robert Murray McCheyne

A sermon that has more head infused into it than heart will not come home with efficacy to the hearers.
—Richard Cecil

Prayer, with its manifold and many-sided forces, helps the mouth to utter the truth in its fullness and freedom. The preacher is to be prayed for, the preacher is made by prayer. The preacher's mouth is to be prayed for; his mouth is to be opened and filled by prayer. A holy mouth is made by praying, by much praying; a brave mouth is made by praying, by much praying. The Church and the world, God and heaven, owe much to Paul's mouth; Paul's mouth owed its power to prayer.

How manifold, illimitable, valuable, and helpful prayer is to the preacher in so many ways, at so many points, in every way! One great value is, it helps his heart.

Praying makes the preacher a heart preacher. Prayer puts the preacher's heart into the preacher's sermon; prayer puts the preacher's sermon into the preacher's heart.

The heart makes the preacher. Men of great hearts are great preachers. Men of bad hearts may do a measure of good, but this is rare. The hireling and the stranger may help the sheep at some points, but it is the good shepherd with the good shepherd's heart who will bless the sheep and answer the full measure of the shepherd's place.

We have emphasized sermon-preparation until we have lost sight of the important thing to be prepared — the heart. A prepared heart is much better than a prepared sermon. A prepared heart will make a prepared sermon.

Volumes have been written laying down the mechanics and taste of sermon-making, until we have become possessed with the idea that this scaffolding is the building. The young preacher has been taught to lay out all his strength on the form, taste, and beauty of his sermon as a mechanical and intellectual product. We have thereby cultivated a vicious taste among the people and raised the clamor for talent instead of grace, eloquence instead of piety, rhetoric instead of revelation, reputation and brilliancy instead of holiness. By it we have lost the true idea of preaching, lost preaching power, lost pungent conviction for sin, lost the rich experience and elevated Christian character, lost the authority over consciences and lives which always results from genuine preaching.

It would not do to say that preachers study too much. Some of them do not study at all; others do not study enough. Numbers do not study the right way to show themselves workmen approved of God. But our great lack is not in head culture, but in heart culture; not lack of knowledge but lack of holiness is our sad and telling defect — not that we know too much, but that we do not meditate on God and his word and watch and fast and pray enough. The heart is the great hindrance to our preaching. Words pregnant with divine truth find in our hearts nonconductors; arrested, they fall shorn and powerless.

Can ambition, that lusts after praise and place, preach the gospel of Him who made himself of no reputation and took on Him the form of a servant? Can the proud, the vain, the egotistical preach the gospel of Him who was meek and lowly? Can the bad-tempered, passionate, selfish, hard, worldly man preach the system which teems with long-suffering, self-denial, tenderness, which imperatively demands separation from enmity and crucifixion to the world? Can the hireling official, heartless, perfunctory, preach the gospel which demands the shepherd to give his life for the sheep? Can the covetous man, who counts salary and money, preach the gospel till he has gleaned his heart and can say in the spirit of Christ and Paul in the words of Wesley: "I count it dung and dross; I trample it under my feet; I (yet not I, but the grace of God in me) esteem it just as the mire of the streets, I desire it not, I seek it not"? God's revelation does not need the light of human genius, the polish and strength of human culture, the brilliancy of human thought, the force of human brains to adorn or enforce it; but it does demand the simplicity, the docility, humility, and faith of a child's heart.

It was this surrender and subordination of intellect and genius to the divine and spiritual forces which made Paul peerless among the apostles. It was this which gave Wesley his power and radicated his labors in the history of humanity. This gave to Loyola the strength to arrest the retreating forces of Catholicism.

Our great need is heart-preparation. Luther held it as an axiom: "He who has prayed well has studied well." We do not say that men are not to think and use their intellects; but he will use his intellect best who cultivates his heart most. We do not say that preachers should not be students; but we do say that their great study should be the Bible, and he studies the Bible best who has kept his heart with diligence. We do not say that the preacher should not know men, but he will be the greater adept in human nature who has fathomed the depths and intricacies of his own heart. We do say that while the channel of preaching is the mind, its fountain is the heart; you may broaden and deepen the channel, but if you do not look well to the purity and depth of the fountain, you will have a dry or polluted channel. We do say that almost any man of common intelligence has sense enough to preach the gospel, but very few have grace enough to do so. We do say that he who has struggled with his own heart and conquered it; who has taught it humility, faith, love, truth, mercy, sympathy, courage; who can pour the rich treasures of the heart thus trained, through a manly intellect, all surcharged with the power of the gospel on the consciences of his hearers — such a one will be the truest, most successful preacher in the esteem of his Lord.

13 Grace from the Heart Rather than the Head

Study not to be a fine preacher, Jerichos are blown down with rams' horns. Look simply unto Jesus for preaching food; and what is wanted will be given, and what is given will be blessed, whether it be a barley grain or a wheaten loaf, a crust or a crumb. Your mouth will be a flowing stream or a fountain sealed, according as your heart is. Avoid all controversy in preaching, talking, or writing; preach nothing down but the devil, and nothing up but Jesus Christ. —Berridge

The heart is the saviour of the world. Heads do not save. Genius, brains, brilliancy, strength, natural gifts do not save. The gospel flows through hearts. All the mightiest forces are heart forces. All the sweetest and loveliest graces are heart graces. Great hearts make great characters; great hearts make divine characters.

God is love. There is nothing greater than love, nothing greater than God. Hearts make heaven; heaven is love. There is nothing higher, nothing sweeter, than heaven. It is the heart and not the head which makes God's great preachers. The heart counts much every way in religion. The heart must speak from the pulpit. The heart must hear in the pew. In fact, we serve God with our hearts. Head homage does not pass current in heaven.

We believe that one of the serious and most popular errors of the modern pulpit is the putting of more thought than prayer, of more head than of heart in its sermons. Big hearts make big preachers; good hearts make good preachers. A theological school to enlarge and cultivate the heart is the golden desideratum of the gospel. The pastor binds his people to him and rules his people by his heart. They may admire his gifts, they may be proud of his ability, they may be affected for the time by his sermons; but the stronghold of his power is his heart. His scepter is love. The throne of his power is his heart.

The good shepherd gives his life for the sheep. Heads never make martyrs. It is the heart which surrenders the life to love and fidelity. It takes great courage to be a faithful pastor, but the heart alone can supply this courage. Gifts and genius may be brave, but it is the gifts and genius of the heart and not of the head.

It is easier to fill the head than it is to prepare the heart. It is easier to make a brain sermon than a heart sermon. It was heart that drew the Son of God from heaven. It is heart that will draw men to heaven. Men of heart is what the world needs to sympathize with its woe, to kiss away its sorrows, to compassionate its misery, and to alleviate its pain. Christ was eminently the man of sorrows, because he was preeminently the man of heart.

"Give me thy heart," is God's requisition of men.

"Give me thy heart!" is man's demand of man.

A professional ministry is a heartless ministry. When salary plays a great part in the ministry, the heart plays little part. We may make preaching our business, and not put our hearts in the business. He who puts self to the front in his preaching puts heart to the rear. He who does not sow with his heart in his study will never reap a harvest for God. The closet is the heart's study. We will learn more about how to preach and what to preach there than we can learn in our libraries. "Jesus wept" is the shortest and biggest verse in the Bible. It is he who goes forth *weeping* (not preaching great sermons), bearing precious seed, who shall come again rejoicing, bringing his sheaves with him.

Praying gives sense, brings wisdom, broadens and strengthens the mind. The closet is a perfect school-teacher and school-house for the preacher. Thought is not only brightened and clarified in prayer, but thought is born in prayer. We can learn more in an hour praying, when praying indeed, than from many hours in the study. Books are in the closet which can be found and read nowhere else. Revelations are made in the closet which are made nowhere else.

14 Unction a Necessity

One bright benison which private prayer brings down upon the ministry is an indescribable and inimitable something — an unction from the Holy One ... If the anointing which we bear come not from the Lord of hosts, we are deceivers, since only in prayer can we obtain it. Let us continue instant, constant, fervent in supplication. Let your fleece lie on the thrashing floor of supplication till it is wet with the dew of heaven.
—Charles Haddon Spurgeon

Alexander Knox, a Christian philosopher of the days of Wesley, not an adherent but a strong personal friend of Wesley, and with much spiritual sympathy with the Wesleyan movement, writes: "It is strange and lamentable, but I verily believe the fact to be that except among Methodists and Methodistical clergymen, there is not much interesting preaching in England. The clergy, too generally, have absolutely lost the art. There is, I conceive, in the great laws of the moral world a kind of secret understanding like the affinities in chemistry, between rightly promulgated religious truth and the deepest feelings of the human mind. Where the one is duly exhibited, the other will respond. Did not our hearts burn within us? — but to this devout feeling is indispensable in the speaker. Now, I am obliged to state from my own observation that this *onction,* as the French not unfitly term it, is beyond all comparison more likely to be found in England in a Methodist conventicle than in a parish Church. This, and this alone, seems really to be that which fills the Methodist houses and thins the Churches. I am, I verily think, no enthusiast; I am a most sincere and cordial churchman, a humble disciple of the School of Hale and Boyle, of Burnet and Leighton. Now I must aver that when I was in this country, two years ago, I did not hear a single preacher who taught me like my own great masters but such as are deemed Methodistical. And I now despair of getting an atom of heart-instruction from any other quarter. The Methodist preachers (however I may not always approve of all their expressions) do most assuredly diffuse this true religion and undefiled. I felt real pleasure last Sunday. I can bear witness that the preacher did at once speak the words of truth and soberness. There was no eloquence — the honest man never dreamed of such a thing — but there was far better: a cordial communication of vitalized truth. I say vitalized because what he declared to others it was impossible not to feel he lived on himself.''

This unction is the art of preaching. The preacher who never had this unction never had the art of preaching. The preacher who has lost this unction has lost the art of preaching. Whatever other arts he may have and retain — the art of sermon-making, the art of eloquence, the art of great, clear thinking, the art of pleasing an audience — he has lost the divine art of preaching. This unction makes God's truth powerful and interesting, draws and attracts, edifies, convicts, saves.

This unction vitalizes God's revealed truth, makes it living and life-giving. Even God's truth spoken without this unction is light, dead, and deadening. Though abounding in truth, though weighty with thought, though sparkling with rhetoric, though pointed by logic, though powerful by earnestness, without this divine unction it issues in death and not in life. Mr. Spurgeon says: "I wonder how long we might beat our brains before we could plainly put into word what is meant by preaching with unction. Yet he who preaches knows its presence, and he who hears soon detects its absence. Samaria, in famine, typifies a discourse without it. Jerusalem, with her feast of fat things full of marrow, may represent a sermon enriched with it. Every one knows what the freshness of the morning is when orient pearls abound on every blade of grass, but who can describe it, much less produce it of itself? Such is the mystery of spiritual anointing. We know, but we cannot tell to others what it is. It is as easy as it is foolish, to counterfeit it. Unction is a thing which you cannot manufacture, and its counterfeits are worse than worthless. Yet it is, in itself, priceless, and beyond measure needful if you would edify believers and bring sinners to Christ."

15 Unction, the Mark of True Gospel Preaching

Speak for eternity. Above all things, cultivate your own spirit. A word spoken by you when your conscience is clear and your heart full of God's Spirit is worth ten thousand words spoken in unbelief and sin. Remember that God, and not man, must have the glory. If the veil of the world's machinery were lifted off, how much we would find is done in answer to the prayers of God's children. —Robert Murray McCheyne

Unction is that indefinable, indescribable something which an old, renowned Scotch preacher describes thus: "There is sometimes somewhat in preaching that cannot be ascribed either to matter or expression, and cannot be described what it is, or from whence it cometh, but with a sweet violence it pierceth into the heart and affections and comes immediately from the Lord; but if there be any way to obtain such a thing, it is by the heavenly disposition of the speaker."

We call it unction. It is this unction which makes the word of God "quick and powerful, and sharper than any two-edged sword, piercing even to the dividing asunder of soul and spirit, and of the joints and marrow, and a discerner of the thoughts and intents of the heart." It is this unction which gives the words of the preacher such point, sharpness, and power, and which creates such friction and stir in many a dead congregation. The same truths have been told in the strictness of the letter, smooth as human oil could make them; but no signs of life, not a pulse throb; all as peaceful as the grave and as dead. The same preacher in the meanwhile receives a baptism of this unction, the divine inflatus is on him, the letter of the Word has been embellished and fired by this mysterious power, and the throbbings of life begin — life which receives or life which resists. The unction pervades and convicts the conscience and breaks the heart.

This divine unction is the feature which separates and distinguishes true gospel preaching from all other methods of presenting the truth, and which creates a wide spiritual chasm between the preacher who has it and the one who has it not. It backs and impregns revealed truth with all the energy of God. Unction is simply putting God in his own word and on his own preacher. By mighty and great prayerfulness and by continual prayerfulness, it is all potential and personal to the preacher; it inspires and clarifies his intellect, gives insight and grasp and projecting power; it gives to the preacher heart power, which is greater than head power; and tenderness, purity, force flow from the heart by it. Enlargement, freedom, fullness of thought, directness and simplicity of utterance are the fruits of this unction.

Often earnestness is mistaken for this unction. He who has the divine unction will be earnest in the very spiritual nature of things, but there may be a vast deal of earnestness without the least mixture of unction.

Earnestness and unction look alike from some points of view. Earnestness may be readily and without detection substituted or mistaken for unction. It requires a spiritual eye and a spiritual taste to discriminate.

Earnestness may be sincere, serious, ardent, and persevering. It goes at a thing with good will, pursues it with perseverance, and urges it with ardor; puts force in it. But all these forces do not rise higher than the mere human. The *man* is in it — the whole man, with all that he has of will and heart, of brain and genius, of planning and working and talking. He has set himself to some purpose which has mastered him, and he pursues to master it. There may be none of God in it. There may be little of God in it, because there is so much of the man in it. He may present pleas in advocacy of his earnest purpose which please or touch and move or overwhelm with conviction of their importance; and in all this earnestness may move along earthly ways, being propelled by human forces only, its altar made by earthly hands and its fire kindled by earthly flames. It is said of a rather famous preacher of gifts, whose construction of Scripture was to his fancy or purpose, that he "grew very eloquent over his own exegesis." So men grow exceeding earnest over their own plans or movements. Earnestness may be selfishness simulated.

What of unction? It is the indefinable in preaching which makes it preaching. It is that which distinguishes and separates preaching from all mere human addresses. It is the divine in preaching. It makes the preaching sharp to those who need sharpness. It distills as the dew to those who need to be refreshed. It is well described as:

"a two-edged sword
Of heavenly temper keen,
And double were the wounds it made
Where'er it glanced between.
'Twas death to sin; 'twas life
To all who mourned for sin.
It kindled and it silenced strife,
Made war and peace within."

This unction comes to the preacher not in the study but in the closet. It is heaven's distillation in answer to prayer. It is the sweetest exhalation of the Holy Spirit. It impregnates, suffuses, softens, percolates, cuts, and soothes. It carries the Word like dynamite, like salt, like sugar; makes the Word a soother, an arraigner, a revealer, a searcher; makes the hearer a culprit or a saint, makes him weep like a child and live like a giant; opens his heart and his purse as gently, yet as strongly as the spring opens the leaves. This unction is not the gift of genius. It is not found in the halls of learning. No eloquence can woo it. No industry can win it. No prelatical hands can confer it. It is the gift of God — the signet set to his own messengers. It is heaven's knighthood given to the chosen true and brave ones who have sought this anointed honor through many an hour of tearful, wrestling prayer.

Earnestness is good and impressive; genius is gifted and great. Thought kindles and inspires, but it takes a diviner endowment, a more powerful energy than earnestness or genius or thought to break the chains of sin, to win estranged and depraved hearts to God, to repair the breaches and restore the Church to her old ways of purity and power. Nothing but this holy unction can do this.

16 Much Prayer the Price of Unction

*All the minister's efforts will be vanity or worse
than vanity if he have not unction. Unction must come
down from heaven and spread a savor and feeling and
relish over his ministry; and among the other means of
qualifying himself for his office, the Bible must hold the
first place, and the last also must be given to the Word
of God and prayer.* — Richard Cecil

In the Christian system unction is the anointing of the
Holy Ghost, separating unto God's work and qualifying
for it. This unction is the one divine enablement by
which the preacher accomplishes the peculiar and saving
ends of preaching. Without this unction there are no
true spiritual results accomplished; the results and
forces in preaching do not rise above the results of unsanctified speech. Without unction the former is as po-

tent as the pulpit.

This divine unction on the preacher generates through the Word of God the spiritual results that flow from the gospel; and without this unction, these results are not secured. Many pleasant impressions may be made, but these all fall far below the ends of gospel preaching. This unction may be simulated. There are many things that look like it, there are many results that resemble its effects; but they are foreign to its results and to its nature. The fervor or softness excited by a pathetic or emotional sermon may look like the movements of the divine unction, but they have no pungent, penetrating, heart-breaking force. No heart-healing balm is there in these surface, sympathetic, emotional movements; they are not radical, neither sin-searching nor sin-curing.

This divine unction is the one distinguishing feature that separates true gospel preaching from all other methods of presenting truth. It backs and interpenetrates the revealed truth with all the force of God. It illumines the Word and broadens and enriches the intellect and empowers it to grasp and apprehend the Word. It qualifies the preacher's heart, and brings it to that condition of tenderness, of purity, of force and light that are necessary to secure the highest results. This unction gives to the preacher liberty and enlargement of thought and soul — a freedom, fullness, and directness of utterance that can be secured by no other process.

Without this unction on the preacher the gospel has no more power to propagate itself than any other system of truth. This is the seal of its divinity. Unction in the preacher puts God in the gospel. Without the unction, God is absent, and the gospel is left to the low and unsatisfactory forces that the ingenuity, interest, or talents of men can devise to enforce and project its doctrines.

It is in this element that the pulpit oftener fails than in any other element. Just at this all-important point it lapses. Learning it may have, brilliancy and eloquence may delight and charm, sensation or less offensive methods may bring the populace in crowds, mental power may impress and enforce truth with all its resources; but without this unction, each and all these will be but as the fretful assault of the waters on a Gibraltar. Spray and foam may cover and spangle; but the rocks are there still, unimpressed and unimpressible. The human heart can no more be swept of its hardness and sin by these human forces than these rocks can be swept away by the ocean's ceaseless flow.

This unction is the consecration force, and its presence the continuous test of that consecration. It is this divine anointing on the preacher that secures his consecration to God and his work. Other forces and motives may call him to the work, but this only is consecration. A separation to God's work by the power of the Holy Spirit is the only consecration recognized by God as legitimate.

The unction, the divine unction, this heavenly anointing, is what the pulpit needs and must have. This divine and heavenly oil put on it by the imposition of God's hand must soften and lubricate the whole man — heart, head, spirit — until it separates him with a mighty separation from all earthly, secular, worldly, selfish motives and aims, separating him to everything that is pure and Godlike.

It is the presence of this unction on the preacher that creates the stir and friction in many a congregation. The same truths have been told in the strictness of the letter, but no ruffle has been seen, no pain or pulsation felt. All is quiet as a graveyard. Another preacher comes, and this mysterious influence is on him; the letter of the Word has been fired by the Spirit, the throes of a mighty movement are felt, it is the unction that pervades and stirs the conscience and breaks the heart. Unctionless preaching makes everything hard, dry, acrid, dead.

This unction is not a memory or an era of the past only; it is a present, realized, conscious fact. It belongs to the experience of the man as well as to his preaching. It is that which transforms him into the image of his divine Master, as well as that by which he declares the truths of Christ with power. It is so much the power in the ministry as to make all else seem feeble and vain without it, and by its presence to atone for the absence of all other and feebler forces.

This unction is not an inalienable gift. It is a conditional gift, and its presence is perpetuated and increased by the same process by which it was at first secured; by unceasing prayer to God, by impassioned desires after God, by estimating it, by seeking it with tireless ardor, by deeming all else loss and failure without it.

How and whence comes this unction? Direct from God in answer to prayer. Praying hearts only are the hearts filled with this holy oil; praying lips only are anointed with this divine unction.

Prayer, much prayer, is the price of preaching unction; prayer, much prayer, is the one, sole condition of keeping this unction. Without unceasing prayer the unction never comes to the preacher. Without perseverance in prayer, the unction, like the manna overkept, breeds worms.

17 Prayer Marks Spiritual Leadership

*Give me one hundred preachers who fear nothing
but sin and desire nothing but God, and I care not a
straw whether they be clergymen or laymen; such alone
will shake the gates of hell and set up the kingdom of
heaven on earth. God does nothing but in answer to
prayer.* —John Wesley

The apostles knew the necessity and worth of prayer
to their ministry. They knew that their high commission
as apostles, instead of relieving them from the necessity
of prayer, committed them to it by a more urgent need;
so that they were exceedingly jealous else some other important work should exhaust their time and prevent their
praying as they ought; so they appointed laymen to look
after the delicate and engrossing duties of ministering to
the poor, that they (the apostles) might, unhindered,

"give themselves continually to prayer and to the ministry of the word." Prayer is put first, and their relation to prayer is put most strongly — "give themselves to it," making a business of it, surrendering themselves to praying, putting fervor, urgency, perseverance, and time in it.

How holy, apostolic men devoted themselves to this divine work of prayer! "Night and day praying exceedingly," says Paul. "We will give ourselves continually to prayer" is the consensus of apostolic devotement. How these New Testament preachers laid themselves out in prayer for God's people! How they put God in full force into their Churches by their praying! These holy apostles did not vainly fancy that they had met their high and solemn duties by delivering faithfully God's word, but their preaching was made to stick and tell by the ardor and insistence of their praying. Apostolic praying was as taxing, toilsome, and imperative as apostolic preaching. They prayed mightily day and night to bring the people to the highest regions of faith and holiness. They prayed mightier still to hold them to this high spiritual altitude. The preacher who has never learned in the school of Christ the high and divine art of intercession for his people will never learn the art of preaching, though homiletics be poured into him by the ton, and though he be the most gifted genius in sermon-making and sermon-delivery.

The prayers of apostolic, saintly leaders do much in making saints of those who are not apostles. If the Church leaders in after years had been as particular and fervent in praying for their people as the apostles were, the sad, dark times of worldliness and apostasy had not marred the history and eclipsed the glory and arrested the advance of the Church. Apostolic praying makes apostolic saints and keeps apostolic times of purity and power in the Church.

What loftiness of soul, what purity and elevation of motive, what unselfishness, what self-sacrifice, what exhaustive toil, what ardor of spirit, what divine tact are requisite to be an intercessor for men!

The preacher is to lay himself out in prayer for his people; not that they might be saved, simply, but that they be mightily saved. The apostles laid themselves out in prayer that their saints might be perfect; not that they should have a little relish for the things of God, but that they "might be filled with all the fullness of God." Paul did not rely on his apostolic preaching to secure this end, but "for this cause he bowed his knees to the Father of our Lord Jesus Christ." Paul's praying carried Paul's converts farther along the highway of sainthood than Paul's preaching did. Epaphras did as much or more by prayer for the Colossian saints than by his preaching. He labored fervently always in prayer for them that "they might stand perfect and complete in all the will of God."

Preachers are preeminently God's leaders. They are primarily responsible for the condition of the Church. They shape its character, give tone and direction to its life.

Much every way depends on these leaders. They shape the times and the institutions. The Church is divine, the treasure it incases is heavenly, but it bears the imprint of the human. The treasure is in earthen vessels, and it smacks of the vessel. The Church of God makes, or is made by, its leaders. Whether it makes them or is made by them, it will be what its leaders are; spiritual if they are so, secular if they are, conglomerate if its leaders are. Israel's kings gave character to Israel's piety. A Church rarely revolts against or rises above the religion of its leaders. Strongly spiritual leaders; men of holy might, at the lead, are tokens of God's favor; disaster and weakness follow the wake of feeble or worldly leaders. Israel had fallen low when God gave children to be their princes and babes to rule over them. No happy state is predicted by the prophets when children oppress God's Israel and women rule over them. Times of spiritual leadership are times of great spiritual prosperity to the Church.

Prayer is one of the eminent characteristics of strong spiritual leadership. Men of mighty prayer are men of might and mold things. Their power with God has the conquering tread.

How can a man preach who does not get his message fresh from God in the closet? How can he preach without having his faith quickened, his vision cleared, and his heart warmed by his closeting with God? Alas, for the pulpit lips which are untouched by this closet flame. Dry and unctionless they will ever be, and truths divine will never come with power from such lips. As far as the real interests of religion are concerned, a pulpit without a closet will always be a barren thing.

A preacher may preach in an official, entertaining, or learned way without prayer, but between this kind of preaching and sowing God's precious seed with holy hands and prayerful, weeping hearts there is an immeasurable distance.

A prayerless ministry is the undertaker for all God's truth and for God's Church. He may have the most costly casket and the most beautiful flowers, but it is a funeral, notwithstanding the charmful array. A prayerless Christian will never learn God's truth; a prayerless ministry will never be able to teach God's truth. Ages of millennial glory have been lost by a prayerless Church. The coming of our Lord has been postponed indefinitely by a prayerless Church. Hell has enlarged herself and filled her dire caves in the presence of the dead service of a prayerless Church.

The best, the greatest offering is an offering of prayer.

If the preachers of the twentieth century will learn well the lesson of prayer, and use fully the power of prayer, the millennium will come to its noon ere the century closes. "Pray without ceasing" is the trumpet call to the preachers of the twentieth century. If the twentieth century will get their texts, their thoughts, their words, their sermons in their closets, the next century will find a new heaven and a new earth. The old sin-stained and sin-eclipsed heaven and earth will pass away under the power of a praying ministry.

18 Preachers Need the Prayers of the People

If some Christians that have been complaining of their ministers had said and acted less before men and had applied themselves with all their might to cry to God for their ministers — had, as it were, risen and stormed heaven with their humble, fervent, and incessant prayers for them — they would have been much more in the way of success. —Jonathan Edwards

Somehow the practice of praying in particular for the preacher has fallen into disuse or become discounted. Occasionally have we heard the practice arraigned as a disparagement of the ministry, being a public declaration by those who do it of the inefficiency of the ministry. It offends the pride of learning and self-sufficiency, perhaps, and these ought to be offended and rebuked in a ministry that is so derelict as to allow them to exist.

Prayer, to the preacher, is not simply the duty of his profession, a privilege, but it is a necessity. Air is not more necessary to the lungs than prayer is to the preacher. It is absolutely necessary for the preaher to pray. It is an absolute necessity that the preacher be prayed for. These two propositions are wedded into a union which ought never to know any divorce: *the preacher must pray; the preacher must be prayed for.* It will take all the praying he can do, and all the praying he can get done, to meet the fearful responsibilities and gain the largest, truest success in his great work. The true preacher, next to the cultivation of the spirit and fact of prayer in himself, in their intensest form, covets with a great covetousness the prayers of God's people.

The holier a man is, the more does he estimate prayer; the clearer does he see that God gives himself to the praying ones, and that the measure of God's revelation to the soul is the measure of the soul's longing, importunate prayer for God. Salvation never finds its way to a prayerless heart. The Holy Spirit never abides in a prayerless spirit. Preaching never edifies a prayerless soul. Christ knows nothing of prayerless Christians. The gospel cannot be projected by a prayerless preacher. Gifts, talents, education, eloquence, God's call, cannot abate the demand of prayer, but only intensify the necessity for the preacher to pray and to be prayed for. The more the preacher's eyes are opened to the nature, responsibility, and difficulties in his work, the more will he see, and if he be a true preacher the more will he feel, the necessity of prayer; not only the increasing demand to pray himself, but to call on others to help him by their prayers.

Paul is an illustration of this. If any man could project the gospel by dint of personal force, by brain power, by culture, by personal grace, by God's apostolic commission, God's extraordinary call, that man was Paul. That the preacher must be a man given to prayer, Paul is an eminent example. That the true apostolic preacher must have the prayers of other good people to give to his ministry its full quota of success, Paul is a pre-eminent example. He asks, he covets, he pleads in an impassioned way for the help of all God's saints. He knew that in the spiritual realm, as elsewhere, in union there is strength; that the concentration and aggregation of faith, desire, and prayer increased the volume of spiritual force until it became overwhelming and irresistible in its power. Units of prayer combined, like drops of water, make an ocean which defies resistance. So Paul, with his clear and full apprehension of spiritual dynamics, determined to make his ministry as impressive, as eternal, as irresistible as the ocean, by gathering all the scattered units of prayer and precipitating them on his ministry. May not the solution of Paul's preeminence in labors and results, and impress on the Church and the world, be found in this fact that he was able to center on himself and his ministry more of prayer than others? To his brethren at Rome he wrote: "Now I beseech you, brethren, for the Lord Jesus Christ's sake, and for the love of the Spirit, that ye strive together with me in prayers to God for me." To the Ephesians he says: "Praying always with all prayer and supplication in the Spirit, and watching thereunto with all perseverance and supplication for all saints; and for me, that utterance may be given unto me, that I may open my mouth boldly, to make known the mystery of the gospel." To the Colossians he emphasizes: "Withal praying also for us, that God would open unto us a door of utterance, to speak the mystery of Christ, for which I am also in bonds: that I may make it manifest as I ought to speak." To the Thessalonians he says sharply, strongly: "Brethren, pray for us." Paul calls on the rinthian Church to help him: "Ye also helping together by prayer for us." This was to be part of their work. They were to lay to the helping hand of prayer. He in an additional and closing charge to the Thessalonian Church about the importance and necessity of their prayers says: "Finally, brethren, pray for us, that the word of the Lord may have free course, and be glorified, even as it is with you: and that we may be delivered from unreasonable and wicked men." He impresses the Philippians that all his trials and opposition can be made subservient to the spread of the gospel by the efficiency of their prayers for him. Philemon was to prepare a lodging for him, for through Philemon's prayer Paul was to be his guest.

Paul's attitude on this question illustrates his humility and his deep insight into the spiritual forces which project the gospel. More than this, it teaches a lesson for all times, that if Paul was so dependent on the prayers of God's saints to give his ministry success, how much greater the necessity that the prayers of God's saints be centered on the ministry of today!

Paul did not feel that this urgent plea for prayer was to lower his dignity, lessen his influence, or depreciate his piety. What if it did? Let dignity go, let influence be destroyed, let his reputation be marred — he must have their prayers. Called, commissioned, chief of the Apostles as he was, all his equipment was imperfect without the prayers of his people. He wrote letters everywhere, urging them to pray for him. Do you pray for your preacher? Do you pray for him in secret? Public prayers are of little worth unless they are founded on or followed up by private praying. The praying ones are to the preacher as Aaron and Hur were to Moses. They hold up his hands and decide the issue that is so fiercely raging around them.

The plea and purpose of the apostles were to put the Church to praying. They did not ignore the grace of cheerful giving. They were not ignorant of the place which religious activity and work occupied in the spiritual life; but not one nor all of these, in apostolic estimate or urgency, could at all compare in necessity and importance with prayer. The most sacred and urgent pleas were used, the most fervid exhortations, the most comprehensive and arousing words were uttered to enforce the all-important obligation and necessity of prayer.

"Put the saints everywhere to praying" is the burden of the apostolic effort and the keynote of apostolic success. Jesus Christ had striven to do this in the days of his personal ministry. As he was moved by infinite compassion at the ripened fields of earth perishing for lack of laborers — and pausing in his own praying — he tries to awaken the stupid sensibilities of his disciples to the duty of prayer as he charges them, "Pray ye the Lord of the harvest that he will send forth laborers into his harvest." "And he spake a parable unto them to this end, that men ought always to pray and not to faint."

19 Deliberation Necessary to Largest Results from Prayer

This perpetual hurry of business and company ruins me in soul if not in body. More solitude and earlier hours! I suspect I have been allotting habitually too little time to religious exercises, as private devotion and religious meditation, Scripture-reading, etc. Hence I am lean and cold and hard. I had better allot two hours or an hour and a half daily. I have been keeping too late hours, and hence have had but a hurried half hour in a morning to myself. Surely the experience of all good men confirms the proposition that without a due measure of private devotions the soul will grow lean. But all may be done through prayer — almighty prayer, I am ready to say — and why not? For that it is almighty is only through the gracious ordination of the God of love and truth. O then, pray, pray, pray! —William Wilberforce

Our devotions are not measured by the clock, but time is of their essence. The ability to wait and stay and press belongs essentially to our intercourse with God. Hurry, everywhere unseeming and damaging, is so to an alarming extent in the great business of communion with God. Short devotions are the bane of deep piety. Calmness, grasp, strength, are never the companions of hurry. Short devotions deplete spiritual vigor, arrest spiritual progress, sap spiritual foundations, blight the root and bloom of spiritual life. They are the prolific source of backsliding, the sure indication of a superficial piety; they deceive, blight, rot the seed, and impoverish the soil.

It is true that Bible prayers in word and print are short, but the praying men of the Bible were with God through many a sweet and holy wrestling hour. They won by few words but long waiting. The prayers Moses records may be short, but Moses prayed to God with fastings and mighty cryings forty days and nights.

The staement of Elijah's praying may be condensed to a few brief paragraphs, but doubtless Elijah, who when "praying he prayed," spent many hours of fiery struggle and lofty intercourse with God before he could, with assured boldness, say to Ahab, "There shall not be dew nor rain these years, but according to my word." The verbal brief of Paul's prayers is short, but Paul "prayed night and day exceedingly." The "Lord's Prayer" is a divine epitome for infant lips, but the man Christ Jesus prayed many an all-night ere His work was done; and His all-night and long-sustained devotions gave to His work its finish and perfection, and to His character the fullness and glory of its divinity.

Spiritual work is taxing work, and men are loath to do it. Praying, true praying, costs an outlay of serious attention and of time, which flesh and blood do not relish. Few persons are made of such strong fiber that they will make a costly outlay when surface work will pass as well in the market. We can habituate ourselves to our beggarly praying until it looks well to us, at least it keeps up a decent form and quiets conscience — the deadliest of opiates! We can slight our praying, and not realize the peril till the foundations are gone. Hurried devotions make weak faith, feeble convictions, questionable piety. To be little with God is to be little for God. To cut short the praying makes the whole religious character short, scrimp, niggardly, and slovenly.

It takes good time for the full flow of God into the spirit. Short devotions cut the pipe of God's full flow. It takes time in the secret places to get the full revelation of God. Little time and hurry mar the picture.

Henry Martyn laments that "want of private devotional reading and shortness of prayer through incessant sermon-making had produced much strangeness between God and his soul." He judged that he had dedicated too much time to *public* ministrations and too little to *private* communion with God. He was much impressed to set apart times for fasting and to devote times for solemn prayer. Resulting from this he records: "Was assisted this morning to pray for two hours." Said William Wilberforce, the peer of kings: "I must secure more time for private devotions. I have been living far too public for me. The shortening of private devotions starves the soul; it grows lean and faint. I have been keeping too late hours." Of a failure in Parliament he says: "Let me record my grief and shame, and all, probably, from private devotions having been contracted, and so God let me stumble." More solitude and earlier hours was his remedy.

More time and early hours for prayer would act like magic to revive and invigorate many a decayed spiritual life. More time and early hours for prayer would be manifest in holy living. A holy life would not be so rare or so difficult a thing if our devotions were not so short and hurried. A Christly temper in its sweet and passionless fragrance would not be so alien and hopeless a heritage if our closet stay were lengthened and intensified. We live shabbily because we pray meanly. Plenty of time to feast in our closets will bring marrow and fatness to our lives. Our ability to stay with God in our closet measures our ability to stay with God out of the closet. Hasty closet visits are deceptive defaulting. We are not only deluded by them, but we are losers by them in many ways and in many rich legacies. Tarrying in the closet instructs and wins. We are taught by it, and the greatest victories are often the results of great waiting — waiting till words are exhausted, and silent and patient waiting gains the crown. Jesus Christ asks with an affronted emphasis, "Shall not God avenge his own elect which cry day and night unto him?"

To pray is the greatest thing we can do: and to do it well there must be calmness, time, and deliberation; otherwise it is degraded into the littlest and meanest of things. True praying has the largest results for good; and poor praying, the least. We cannot do too much of real praying; we cannot do too little of the sham. We must learn anew the school of prayer. There is nothing which it takes more time to learn. And if we would learn the wondrous art, we must not give a fragment here and there — "A little talk with Jesus," as the tiny saintlets sing — but we must demand and hold with iron grasp the best hours of the day for God and prayer, or there will be no praying worth the name.

This, however, is not a day of prayer. Few men there are who pray. Prayer is defamed by preacher and priest. In these days of hurry and bustle, of electricity and steam, men will not take time to pray. Preachers there are who "say prayers" as a part of their programme, on regular or state occasions; but who "stirs himself up to

take hold upon God?'' Who prays as Elijah prayed —
till all the locked-up forces of nature were unsealed and
a famine-stricken land bloomed as the garden of God?
Who prayed as Jesus Christ prayed as out upon the
mountain he "continued all night in prayer to God"?
The apostles "gave themselves to prayer" — the most
difficult thing to get men or even the preachers to do.
Laymen there are who will give their money — some of
them in rich abundance — but they will not "give themselves" to prayer, without which their money is but a
curse. There are plenty of preachers who will preach and
deliver great and eloquent addresses on the need of
revival and the spread of the kingdom of God, but not
many there are who will do that without which all
preaching and organizing are worse than vain — pray. It
is out of date, almost a lost art, and the greatest bene-
factor this age could have is the man who will bring the
preachers and the Church back to prayer.

20 A Praying Pulpit Begets a Praying Pew

I judge that my prayer is more than the devil himself; if it were otherwise, Luther would have fared differently long before this. Yet men will not see and acknowledge the great wonders or miracles God works in my behalf. If I should neglect prayer but a single day, I should lose a great deal of the fire of faith.
—Martin Luther

Only glimpses of the great importance of prayer could the apostles get before Pentecost. But the Spirit coming and filling on Pentecost elevated prayer to its vital and all-commanding position in the gospel of Christ. The call now of prayer to every saint is the Spirit's loudest and most exigent call. Sainthood's piety is made, refined, perfected, by prayer. The gospel moves with slow and timid pace when the saints are not at their prayers

93

early and late and long.

Where are the Christly leaders who can teach the modern saints how to pray and put them at it? Do we know we are raising up a prayerless set of saints? Where are the apostolic leaders who can put God's people to praying? Let them come to the front and do the work, and it will be the greatest work which can be done. An increase of educational facilities and a great increase of money force will be the direst curse to religion if they are not sanctified by more and better praying than we are doing. More praying will not come as a matter of course. The campaign for the twentieth or thirtieth century fund will not help our praying but hinder if we are not careful. Nothing but a specific effort from a praying leadership will avail. The chief ones must lead in the apostolic effort to radicate the vital importance and *fact* of prayer in the heart and life of the Church. None but praying leaders can have praying followers. Praying apostles will beget praying saints. A praying pulpit will beget praying pews. We do greatly need somebody who can set the saints to this business of praying. We are not a generation of praying saints. Nonpraying saints are a beggarly gang of saints who have neither the ardor nor the beauty nor the power of saints. Who will restore this breach? The greatest will he be of reformers and apostles, who can set the Church to praying.

We put it as our most sober judgment that the great need of the Church in this and all ages is men of such commanding faith, of such unsullied holiness, of such marked spiritual vigor and consuming zeal, that their prayers, faith, lives, and ministry will be of such a radical and aggressive form as to work spiritual revolutions which will form eras in individual and Church life.

We do not mean men who get up sensational stirs by novel devices, nor those who attract by a pleasing entertainment; but men who can stir things, and work revolu-

tions by the preaching of God's Word and by the power
of the Holy Ghost, revolutions which change the whole
current of things.

Natural ability and educational advantages do not
figure as factors in this matter; but capacity for faith,
the ability to pray, the power of thorough consecration,
the ability of self-littleness, an absolute losing of one's
self in God's glory, and an ever-present and insatiable
yearning and seeking after all the fullness of God —
men who can set the Church ablaze for God; not in a
noisy, showy way, but with an intense and quiet heat
that melts and moves everything for God.

God can work wonders if He can get a suitable man.
Men can work wonders if they can get God to lead
them. The full endowment of the spirit that turned the
world upside down would be eminently useful in these
latter days. Men who can stir things mightily for God,
whose spiritual revolutions change the whole aspect of
things, are the universal need of the Church.

The Church has never been without these men; they
adorn its history; they are the standing miracles of the
divinity of the Church; their example and history are an
unfailing inspiration and blessing. An increase in their
number and power should be our prayer.

That which has been done in spiritual matters can be
done again, and be better done. This was Christ's view.
He said "Verily, verily, I say unto you, He that
believeth on me, the works that I do shall he do also;
and greater works than these shall he do; because I go to
my Father." The past has not exhausted the possibilities
nor the demands for doing great things for God. The
Church that is dependent on its past history for its
miracles of power and grace is a fallen Church.

God wants elect men — men out of whom self and the
world have gone by a severe crucifixion, by a bankruptcy which has so totally ruined self and the world

that there is neither hope nor desire of recovery; men who by this insolvency and crucifixion have turned toward God perfect hearts.

Let us pray ardently that God's promise to prayer may be more than realized.

PURPOSE
IN
PRAYER

I

*My Creed leads me to think that prayer is effica-
cious, and surely a day's asking God to overrule all
events for good is not lost. Still there is a great feeling
that when a man is praying he is doing nothing, and this
feeling makes us give undue importance to work, sometimes even to the hurrying over or even to the neglect of
prayer.*

*Do not we rest in our day too much on the arm of
flesh? Cannot the same wonders be done now as of old?
Do not the eyes of the Lord run to and fro throughout
the whole earth still to show Himself strong on behalf of
those who put their trust in Him? Oh that God would
give me more practical faith in Him! Where is now the
Lord God of Elijah? He is waiting for Elijah to call on
Him.* —James Gilmour of Mongolia

The more praying there is in the world the better the
world will be, the mightier the forces against evil every-

where. Prayer, in one phase of its operation, is a disinfectant and a preventive. It purifies the air; it destroys the contagion of evil. Prayer is no fitful, shortlived thing. It is no voice crying unheard and unheeded in the silence. It is a voice which goes into God's ear, and it lives as long as God's ear is open to holy pleas, as long as God's heart is alive to holy things.

God shapes the world by prayer. Prayers are deathless. The lips that uttered them may be closed in death, the heart that felt them may have ceased to beat, but the prayers live before God, and God's heart is set on them and prayers outlive the lives of those who uttered them; outlive a generation, outlive an age, outlive a world.

That man is the most immortal who has done the most and the best praying. They are God's heroes, God's saints, God's servants, God's vicegerents. A man can pray better because of the prayers of the past; a man can live holier because of the prayers of the past, the man of many and acceptable prayers has done the truest and greatest service to the incoming generation. The prayers of God's saints strengthen the unborn generation against the desolating waves of sin and evil. Woe to the generation of sons who find their censers empty of the rich incense of prayer; whose fathers have been too busy or too unbelieving to pray, and perils inexpressible and consequences untold are their unhappy heritage. Fortunate are they whose fathers and mothers have left them a wealthy patrimony of prayer.

The prayers of God's saints are the capital stock in heaven by which Christ carries on His great work upon earth. The great throes and mighty convulsions on earth are the results of these prayers. Earth is changed, revolutionised, angels move on more powerful, more rapid wing, and God's policy is shaped as the prayers are more numerous, more efficient.

It is true that the mightiest successes that come to God's cause are created and carried on by prayer. God's day of power; the angelic days of activity and power are when God's Church comes into its mightiest inheritance of mightiest faith and mightiest prayer. God's conquering days are when the saints have given themselves to mightiest prayer. When God's house on earth is a house of prayer, then God's house in heaven is busy and all potent in its plans and movements, then His earthly armies are clothed with the triumphs and spoils of victory and His enemies defeated on every hand.

God conditions the very life and prosperity of His cause on prayer. The condition was put in the very existence of God's cause in this world. *Ask of Me* is the one condition God puts in the very advance and triumph of His cause.

Men are to pray — to pray for the advance of God's cause. Prayer puts God in full force in the world. To a prayerful man God is present in realised force; to a prayerful Church God is present in glorious power, and the Second Psalm is the Divine description of the establishment of God's cause through Jesus Christ. All inferior dispensations have merged in the enthronement of Jesus Christ. God declares the enthronement of His Son. The nations are incensed with bitter hatred against His cause. God is described as laughing at their enfeebled hate. The Lord will laugh; The Lord will have them in derision. "Yet have I set My King upon My holy hill of Zion." The decree has passed immutable and eternal:

> I will tell of the decree:
> The Lord said unto Me, Thou art My Son;
> This day have I begotten Thee.
> *Ask of Me,* and I will give Thee the nations
> for Thine inheritance,

7

And the uttermost parts of the earth for Thy
  possession.
Thou shalt break them with a rod of iron;
Thou shalt dash them in pieces like a potter's
  vessel.

Ask of Me is the condition — a praying people willing
and obedient. "And men shall pray for Him continually." Under this universal and simple promise men and
women of old laid themselves out for God. They prayed
and God answered their prayers, and the cause of God
was kept alive in the world by the flame of their praying.
  Prayer became a settled and only condition to move
His Son's Kingdom. "Ask, and ye shall receive; seek,
and ye shall find; knock, and it shall be opened." The
strongest one in Christ's kingdom is he who is the best
knocker. The secret of success in Christ's Kingdom is
the ability to pray. The one who can wield the power of
prayer is the strong one, the holy one in Christ's
Kingdom. The most important lesson we can learn is
how to pray.
  Prayer is the keynote of the most sanctified life, of
the holiest ministry. He does the most for God who is
the highest skilled in prayer. Jesus Christ exercised His
ministry after this order.

II

That we ought to give ourselves to God with regard to things both temporal and spiritual, and seek our satisfaction only in the fulfilling His will, whether He lead us by suffering, or by consolation, for all would be equal to a soul truly resigned. Prayer is nothing else but a sense of God's presence. —Brother Lawrence

Be sure you look to your secret duty; keep that up whatever you do. The soul cannot prosper in the neglect of it. Apostasy generally begins at the closet door. Be much in secret fellowship with God. It is secret trading that enriches the Christian.

Pray alone. Let prayer be the key of the morning and the bolt at night. The best way to fight against sin is to fight it on our knees. —Philip Henry

The prayer of faith is the only power in the universe to which the Great Jehovah yields. Prayer is the sovereign remedy. —Robert Hall

9

An hour of solitude passed in sincere and earnest prayer, or the conflict with and conquest over a single passion or subtle bosom sin will teach us more of thought, will more effectually awaken the faculty and form the habit of reflection than a year's study in the schools without them. —Coleridge

A man may pray night and day and deceive himself, but no man can be assured of his sincerity who does not pray. Prayer is faith passing into act. A union of the will and intellect realising in an intellectual act. It is the whole man that prays. Less than this is wishing or lip work, a sham or a mummery.
If God should restore me again to health I have determined to study nothing but the Bible. Literature is inimical to spirituality if it be not kept under with a firm hand. —Richard Cecil

Our sanctification does not depend upon changing our works, but in doing that for God's sake which we commonly do for our own. The time of business does not with me differ from the time of prayer. Prayer is nothing else but a sense of the presence of God.
—Brother Lawrence

Let me burn out for God. After all, whatever God may appoint, prayer is the great thing. Oh that I may be a man of prayer. —Henry Martyn

The possibilities and necessity of prayer, its power and results are manifested in arresting and changing the purposes of God and in relieving the stroke of His power. Abimelech was smitten by God:

So Abraham prayed unto God: and God healed Abimelech, and his wife, and his maidservants; and they bare *children*.

For the Lord had fast closed up all the wombs of the house of Abimelech, because of Sarah Abraham's wife.

Job's miserable, mistaken, comforters had so deported themselves in their controversy with Job that God's wrath was kindled against them. "My servant Job shall pray for you," said God, "for him will I accept."

"And the Lord turned the captivity of Job when he prayed for his friends."

Jonah was in dire condition when "the Lord sent out a great wind into the sea, and there was a mighty tempest." When lots were cast, "the lot fell upon Jonah." He was cast overboard into the sea, but "the Lord had prepared a great fish to swallow up Jonah ... Then Jonah prayed unto the Lord his God out of the fish's belly ... and the Lord spake unto the fish, and it vomited out Jonah upon the dry land."

When the disobedient prophet lifted up his voice in prayer, God heard and sent deliverance.

Pharoah was a firm believer in the possibilities of prayer, and its ability to relieve. When staggering under the woeful curses of God, he pleaded with Moses to intercede for him. "Intreat the Lord for me," was his pathetic appeal four times repeated when the plagues were scourging Egypt. Four times were these urgent appeals made to Moses, and four times did prayer lift the dread curse from the hard king and his doomed land.

The blasphemy and idolatry of Israel in making the golden calf and declaring their devotions to it were a fearful crime. The anger of God waxed hot, and He declared that He would destroy the offending people.

11

The Lord was very wroth with Aaron also, and to Moses He said, "Let Me alone that I may destroy them." But Moses prayed, and kept on praying; day and night he prayed forty days. He makes the record of his prayer struggle. "I fell down," he says, "before the Lord at the first forty days and nights; I did neither eat bread nor drink water because of your sins which ye sinned in doing wickedly in the sight of the Lord to provoke Him to anger. For I was afraid of the anger and hot displeasure wherewith the Lord was hot against you to destroy you. But the Lord hearkened to me at this time also. And the Lord was very angry with Aaron to have destroyed him. And I prayed for him also at the same time."

"Yet forty days, and Nineveh shall be overthrown. It was the purpose of God to destroy that great and wicked city. But Nineveh prayed, covered with sackcloth; sitting in ashes she cried "mightily to God," and "God repented of the evil that He said He would do unto them; and He did it not."

The message of God to Hezekiah was: "Set thine house in order; for thou shalt die and not live." Hezekiah turned his face toward the wall, and prayed unto the Lord, and said: "Remember now, O Lord, I beseech Thee, how I have walked before Thee in truth, and with a perfect heart, and have done that which is good in Thy sight." And Hezekiah wept sore. God said to Isaiah, "Go, say to Hezekiah, I have heard thy prayer, I have seen thy tears; behold, I will add unto thy days fifteen years."

These men knew how to pray and how to prevail in prayer. Their faith in prayer was no passing attitude that changed with the wind or with their own feelings and circumstances; it was a fact that God heard and answered, that His ear was ever open to the cry of His children, and that the power to do what was asked of

Him was commensurate with His willingness. And thus these men, strong in faith and in prayer, "subdued kingdoms, wrought righteousness, obtained promises, stopped the mouths of lions, quenched the power of fire, escaped the edge of the sword, from weakness were made strong, waxed mighty in war, turned to flight the armies of the aliens."

Everything then, as now, was possible to the men and women who knew how to pray. Prayer, indeed, opened a limitless storehouse, and God's hand withheld nothing. Prayer introduced those who practised it into a world of privilege, and brought the strength and wealth of heaven down to the aid of finite man. What rich and wonderful power was theirs who had learned the secret of victorious approach to God! With Moses it saved a nation; with Ezra it saved a church.

And yet, strange as it seems when we contemplate the wonders of which God's people had been witness, there came a slackness in prayer. The mighty hold upon God, that had so often struck awe and terror into the hearts of their enemies, lost its grip. The people, backslidden and apostate, had gone off from their praying — if the bulk of them had ever truly prayed. The Pharisee's cold and lifeless praying was substituted for any genuine approach to God, and because of that formal method of praying the whole worship became a parody of its real purpose. A glorious dispensation, and gloriously executed, was it by Moses, by Ezra, by Daniel and Elijah, by Hannah and Samuel; but the circle seems limited and shortlived; the praying ones were few and far between. They had no survivors, none to imitate their devotion to God, none to preserve the roll of the elect.

In vain had the decree established the Divine order, the Divine call. *Ask of Me.* From the earnest and fruitful crying to God they turned their faces to pagan gods, and cried in vain for the answers that could never come. And so they sank into that godless and pitiful state that has lost its object in life when the link with the Eternal has been broken. Their favoured dispensation of prayer was forgotten; they knew not how to pray.

What a contrast to the achievements that brighten up other pages of holy writ. The power working through Elijah and Elisha in answer to prayer reached down even to the very grave. In each case a child was raised from the dead, and the powers of famine were broken. "The supplications of a righteous man avail much." Elijah was a man of like passions with us. He prayed fervently that it might not rain, and it rained not on the earth for three years and six months. And he prayed again, and the heaven gave rain, and the earth brought forth her fruit. Jonah prayed while imprisoned in the great fish, and he came to dry land, saved from storm and sea and monsters of the deep by the mighty energy of his praying.

How wide the gracious provision of the grace of praying as administered in that marvellous dispensation. They prayed wondrously. Why could not their praying save the dispensation from decay and death? Was it not because they lost the fire without which all praying degenerates into a lifeless form? It takes effort and toil and care to prepare the incense. Prayer is no laggard's work. When all the rich, spiced graces from the body of prayer have by labour and beating been blended and refined and intermixed, the fire is needed to unloose the incense and make its fragrance rise to the throne of God. The fire that consumes creates the spirit and life of the incense. Without fire prayer has no spirit; it is, like dead spices, for corruption and worms.

The casual, intermittent prayer is never bathed in this Divine fire. For the man who thus prays is lacking in the earnestness that lays hold of God, determined not to let Him go until the blessing comes. "Pray without ceasing," counselled the great Apostle. That is the habit that drives prayer right into the mortar that holds the building stones together. "You can do more than pray after you have prayed," said the godly Dr. A. J. Gordon, "but you cannot do more than pray until you have prayed." The story of every great Christian achievement is the history of answered prayer.

"The greatest and the best talent that God gives to any man or woman in this world is the talent of prayer," writes Principal Alexander Whyte. "And the best usury that any man or woman brings back to God when He comes to reckon with them at the end of this world is a life of prayer. And those servants best put their Lord's money 'to the exchangers' who rise early and sit late, as long as they are in this world, ever finding out and ever following after better and better methods of prayer, and ever forming more secret, more steadfast, and more spiritually fruitful habits of prayer, till they literally 'pray without ceasing,' and till they continually strike out into new enterprises in prayer, and new achievements, and new enrichments."

Martin Luther, when once asked what his plans for the following day were, answered: "Work, work, from early until late. In fact, I have so much to do that I shall spend the first three hours in prayer." Cromwell, too, believed in being much upon his knees. Looking on one occasion at the statues of famous men, he turned to a friend and said: "Make mine kneeling, for thus I came to glory."

It is only when the whole heart is gripped with the passion of prayer that the life-giving fire descends, for none but the earnest man gets access to the ear of God.

III

When thou feelest thyself most indisposed to prayer yield not to it, but strive and endeavor to pray even when thou thinkest thou canst not pray. —Hildersam

It was among the Parthians the custom that none was to give their children any meat in the morning before they saw the sweat on their faces, and you shall find this to be God's usual course not to give His children the taste of His delights till they begin to sweat in seeking after them.
—Richard Baxter

Of all the duties enjoined by Christianity none is more essential and yet more neglected than prayer. Most people consider the exercise a fatiguing ceremony, which they are justified in abridging as much as possible. Even those whose profession or fears lead them to pray, pray with such languor and wanderings of mind that their prayers, far from drawing down blessings, only increase their condemnation. —Fenelon

More praying and better is the secret of the whole matter. More time for prayer, more relish and preparation to meet God, to commune with God through Christ — this has in it the whole of the matter. Our manner and matter of praying ill become us. The attitude and relationship of God and the Son are the eternal relationship of Father and Son, of asking and giving — the Son always asking, the Father always giving:

> *Ask of Me,* and I will give *Thee* the nations for
>   Thine inheritance,
> And the uttermost parts of the earth for Thy
>   possession.
> Thou shalt break them with a rod of iron;
> Thou shalt dash them in pieces like a potter's
>   vessel.

Jesus is to be always praying through His people. "And men shall pray for Him continually." "For My house shall be called a house of prayer for My peoples." We must prepare ourselves to pray; to be like Christ, to pray like Christ.

Man's access in prayer to God opens everything, and makes his impoverishment his wealth. All things are his through prayer. The wealth and the glory — all things are Christ's. As the light grows brighter and prophets take in the nature of the restoration, the Divine record seems to be enlarged. "Thus saith the Lord, the Holy One of Israel and His Maker, ask Me of things that are to come, concerning My sons, and concerning the work of My hands command ye Me. I have made the earth, and created man upon it: I, even My hands, have stretched out the heavens and all their host have I commanded."

To man is given to command God with all this authority

and power in the demands of God's earthly Kingdom. Heaven, with all it has, is under tribute to carry out the ultimate, final and glorious purposes of God. Why then is the time so long in carrying out these wise benedictions for man? Why then does sin so long reign? Why are the oath-bound covenant promises so long in coming to their gracious end? Sin reigns, Satan reigns, sighing marks the lives of many; all tears are fresh and full.

Why is all this so? We have not prayed to bring the evil to an end; we have not prayed as we must pray. We have not met the conditions of prayer.

Ask of Me. Ask of God. We have not rested on prayer. We have not made prayer the sole condition. There has been violation of the primary condition of prayer. We have not prayed aright. We have not prayed at all. God is willing to give, but we are slow to ask. The Son, through His saints, is ever praying and God the Father is ever answering.

Ask of Me. In the invitation is conveyed the assurance of answer; the shout of victory is there and may be heard by the listening ear. The Father holds the authority and power in His hands. How easy is the condition, and yet how long are we in fulfilling the conditions! Nations are in bondage; the uttermost parts of the earth are still unpossessed. The earth groans; the world is still in bondage; Satan and evil hold sway.

The Father holds Himself in the attitude of Giver, *Ask of Me,* and that petition to God the Father empowers all agencies, inspires all movements. The Gospel is Divinely inspired. Back of all its inspirations is prayer. *Ask of Me* lies back of all movements. Standing as the endowment of the enthroned Christ is the oath-bound covenant of the Father, *"Ask of Me,* and I will give thee the nations for thine inheritance, and the uttermost

parts of the earth for thy possession." "And men shall
pray to Him continually."

Ever are the prayers of holy men streaming up to God
as fragrant as the richest incense. And God in many
ways is speaking to us, declaring his wealth and our impoverishment. "I am the Maker of all things; the wealth
and glory are Mine. *Command ye Me.*"

We can do all things by God's aid, and can have the
whole of His aid by asking. The Gospel, in its success
and power, depends on our ability to pray. The dispensations of God depend on man's ability to pray. We can
have all that God has. *Command ye Me.* This is no fig-
ment of the imagination, no idle dream, no vain fancy.
The life of the Church is the highest life. Its office is to
pray. Its prayer life is the highest life, the most odorous,
the most conspicuous.

The Book of Revelation says nothing about prayer as
a great duty, a hallowed service, but much about prayer
in its aggregated force and energies. It is the prayer
force ever living and ever praying; it is all saints' prayers
going out as a mighty, living energy while the lips that
uttered the words are stilled and sealed in death, while
the living church has an energy of faith to inherit the
forces of all the past praying and make it deathless.

The statement by the Baptist philospher, John Foster,
contains the purest philosophy and the simple truth of
God, for God has no force and demands no conditions
but prayer. "More and better praying will bring the
surest and readiest triumph to God's cause; feeble, formal, listless praying brings decay and death. The
Church has its sheet-anchor in the closet; its magazine
stores are there."

"I am convinced," Foster continues, "that every man
who amidst his serious projects is apprized of his dependence upon God as completely as that dependence is a

fact, will be impelled to pray and anxious to induce his serious friends to pray almost every hour. He will not without it promise himself any noble success any more than a mariner would expect to reach a distant coast by having his sails spread in a stagnation of air.

"I have intimated my fear that it is visionary to expect an unusual success in the human administration of religion unless there are unusual omens: now a most emphatical spirit of prayer would be such an omen; and the individual who should determine to try its last possible efficacy might probably find himself becoming a much more prevailing agent in his little sphere. And if the whole, or the greater number of the disciples of Christianity were with an earnest and unalterable resolution of each to combine that heaven should not withhold one single influence which the very utmost effort of conspiring and persevering supplication would obtain, it would be a sign that a revolution of the world was at hand."

Edward Payson, one of God's own, says of this statement of Foster, "Very few missionaries since the apostles, probably have tried the experiment. He who shall make the first trial will, I believe, effect wonders. Nothing that I could write, nothing that an angel could write, would be necessary to him who should make this trial.

"One of the principal results of the little experience which I have had as a Christian minister is a conviction that religion consists very much in giving God that place in our views and feelings which He actually fills in the universe. We know that in the universe He is all in all. So far as He is constantly all in all to us, so far as we comply with the Psalmist's charge to his soul, 'My soul, wait thou *only* upon God;' so far, I apprehend, have we advanced towards perfection. It is comparatively easy to wait upon God; but to wait upon Him *only* — to feel, so far as our strength, happiness, and usefulness are concerned, as if all creatures and second causes were annihilated, and we were alone in the universe with God, is, I suspect, a difficult and rare attainment. At least, I am sure it is one which I am very far from having made. In proportion as we make this attainment we shall find everything easy; for we shall become, emphatically, men of prayer; and we may say of prayer as Solomon says of money, that it answereth all things.''

This same John Foster said, when approaching death: ''I never prayed more earnestly nor probably with such faithful frequency. 'Pray without ceasing' has been the sentence repeating itself in the silent thought, and I am sure it must be my practice till the last conscious hour of life. Oh, why not throughout that long, indolent, inanimate half-century past?''

And yet this is the way in which we all act about prayer. Conscious as we are of its importance, of its vital importance, we yet let the hours pass away as a blank and can only lament in death the irremediable loss.

When we calmly reflect upon the fact that the progress of our Lord's Kingdom is dependent upon prayer, it is sad to think that we give so little time to the holy exercise. Everything depends upon prayer, and yet we neglect it not only to our own spiritual hurt but also to the delay and injury of our Lord's cause upon the earth. The forces of good and evil are contending for the world. If we would, we could add to the conquering power of the army of righteousness, and yet our lips are sealed, our hands hang listlessly by our side, and we jeopardise the very cause in which we profess to be deeply interested by holding back from the prayer chamber.

Prayer is the one prime, eternal condition by which the Father is pledged to put the Son in possession of the world. Christ prays through His people. Had there been importunate, universal and continuous prayer by God's people, long ere this the earth had been possessed for Christ. The delay is not to be accounted for by the inveterate obstacles, but by the lack of the right asking. We do more of everything else than of praying. As poor as our giving is, our contributions of money exceed our offerings of prayer. Perhaps in the average congregation fifty aid in paying, where one saintly, ardent soul shuts itself up with God and wrestles for the deliverance of the heathen world. Official praying on set or state occasions counts for nothing in this estimate. We emphasise other things more than we do the necessity of prayer.

We are saying prayers after an orderly way, but we have not the world in the grasp of our faith. We are not praying after the order that moves God and brings all Divine influences to help us. The world needs more true praying to save it from the reign and ruin of Satan.

We do not pray as Elijah prayed. John Foster puts the whole matter to a practical point. "When the Church of God," he says, "is aroused to its obligation and duties and right faith to claim what Christ has promised — 'all things whatsoever' — a revolution will take place."

But not all praying is praying. The driving power, the conquering force in God's cause is God Himself. "Call upon Me and I will answer thee and show thee great and mighty things which thou knowest not," is God's challenge to prayer. Prayer puts God in full force into God's work. "Ask of Me things to come, concerning My sons, and concerning the work of My hands command ye Me" — God's *carte blanche* to prayer. Faith is only omnipotent when on its knees, and its outstretched hands

23

take hold of God, then it draws to the utmost of God's capacity; for only a praying faith can get God's "all things whatsoever." Wonderful lessons are the Syrophenician woman, the importunate widow, and the friend at midnight, of what dauntless prayer can do in mastering or defying conditions, in changing defeat into victory and triumphing in the regions of despair. Oneness with Christ, the acme of spiritual attainment, is glorious in all things; most glorious in that we can then "ask what we will and it shall be done unto us." Prayer in Jesus' name puts the crowning crown on God, because it glorifies Him through the Son and pledges the Son to give to men "whatsoever and anything" they shall ask.

In the New Testament the marvellous prayer of the Old Testament is put to the front that it may provoke and stimulate our praying, and it is preceded with a declaration, the dynamic energy of which we can scarcely translate. "The supplication of a righteous man availeth much. Elijah was a man of like passions with us, and he prayed earnestly that it might not rain, and it rained not on the earth by the space of three years and six months. And he prayed again, and the heaven gave rain, and the earth brought forth her fruit."

Our paucity in results, the cause of all leanness, is solved by the Apostle James — "Ye have not, because ye ask not. Ye ask and receive not, because ye ask amiss, that ye may spend it on your pleasures."

That is the whole truth in a nutshell.

IV

The potency of prayer hath subdued the strength of fire; it had bridled the rage of lions, hushed the anarchy to rest, extinguished wars, appeased the elements, expelled demons, burst the chains of death, expanded the gates of heaven, assuaged diseases, repelled frauds, rescued cities from destruction, stayed the sun in its course, and arrested the progress of the thunderbolt. Prayer is an all-efficient panoply, a treasure undiminished, a mine which is never exhausted, a sky unobscured by clouds, a heaven unruffled by the storm. It is the root, the fountain, the mother of a thousand blessings.
—Chrysostom

The prayers of holy men appease God's wrath, drive away temptations, resist and overcome the devil, procure the ministry and service of angels, rescind the decrees of God. Prayer cures sickness and obtains pardon; it arrests the sun in its course and stays the wheels of the chariot of the moon; it rules over all gods and

25

opens and shuts the storehouses of rain, it unlocks the cabinet of the womb and quenches the violence of fire; it stops the mouths of lions and reconciles our suffering and weak faculties with the violence of torment and violence of persecution; it pleases God and supplies all our need.—Jeremy Taylor

> *More things are wrought by prayer*
> *Than this world dreams of. Wherefore,*
>   *let thy voice*
> *Rise like a fountain for me night and day.*
> *For what are men better than sheep or goats,*
> *That nourish a blind life within the brain,*
> *If, knowing God, they lift not*
>   *hands of prayer*
> *Both for themselves and those who call them*
>   *friend?*
> *For so the whole round earth is every way*
> *Bound by gold chains about the feet of God.*
>   —Tennyson

Perfect prayer is only another name for love.
                                   —Fenelon

It was said of the late C. H. Spurgeon, that he glided from laughter to prayer with the naturalness of one who lived in both elements. With him the habit of prayer was free and unfettered. His life was not divided into compartments, the one shut off from the other with a rigid exclusiveness that barred all intercommunication. He lived in constant fellowship with his Father in Heaven. He was ever in touch with God, and thus it was as natural for him to pray as it was for him to breathe.

"What a fine time we have had; let us thank God for it," he said to a friend on one occasion, when, out under the blue sky and wrapped in glorious sunshine, they had enjoyed a holiday with the unfettered enthusiasm of schoolboys. Prayer sprang as spontaneously to his lips as did ordinary speech, and never was there the slightest incongruity in his approach to the Divine throne straight from any scene in which he might be taking part.

That is the attitude with regard to prayer that ought to mark every child of God. There are, and there ought to be, stated seasons of communication with God when, everything else shut out, we come into His presence to talk to Him and to let Him speak to us; and out of such seasons springs that beautiful habit of prayer that weaves a golden bond between earth and heaven. Without such stated seasons the habit of prayer can never be formed; without them there is no nourishment for the spiritual life. By means of them the soul is lifted into a new atmosphere — the atmosphere of the heavenly city, in which it is easy to open the heart to God and to speak with Him as friend speaks with friend.

Thus, in every circumstance of life, prayer is the most natural out-pouring of the soul, the unhindered turning to God for communion and direction. Whether in sorrow or in joy, in defeat or in victory, in health or in weakness, in calamity or in success, the heart leaps to meet with God just as a child runs to his mother's arms, ever sure that with her is the sympathy that meets every need.

Dr. Adam Clarke, in his autobiography, records that when Mr. Wesley was returning to England by ship, considerable delay was caused by contrary winds. Wesley was reading, when he became aware of some confusion on board, and asking what was the matter, he was informed that the wind was contrary. "Then," was his reply, "let us go to prayer."

After Dr. Clarke had prayed, Wesley broke out into

fervent supplication which seemed to be more the offering of faith than of mere desire. "Almighty and everlasting God," he prayed. "Thou hast sway everywhere, and all things serve the purpose of Thy will, Thou holdest the winds in Thy fists and sittest upon the water floods, and reignest a King for ever. Command these winds and these waves that they obey Thee, and take us speedily and safely to the haven whither we would go."

The power of this petition was felt by all. Wesley rose from his knees, made no remark, but took up his book and continued reading. Dr. Clarke went on deck, and to his surprise found the vessel under sail, standing on her right course. Nor did she change till she was safely at anchor. On the sudden and favourable change of wind, Wesley made no remark; so fully did he *expect to be heard* that he took it for granted that he *was heard.*

That was prayer with a purpose — the definite and direct utterance of one who knew that he had the ear of God, and that God had the willingness as well as the power to grant the petition which he asked of Him.

Major D. W. Whittle, in an introduction to the wonders of prayer, says of George Muller, of Bristol: "I met Mr. Muller in the express, the morning of our sailing from Quebec to Liverpool. About half-an-hour before the tender was to take the passengers to the ship, he asked of the agent if a deck chair had arrived for him from New York. He was answered, 'No,' and told that it could not possibly come in time for the steamer. I had with me a chair I had just purchased, and told Mr. Muller of the place near by, and suggested, as but a few moments remained, that he had better buy one at once. His reply was, 'No, my brother. Our Heavenly Father will send the chair from New York. It is one used by Mrs. Muller. I wrote ten days ago to a brother, who promised to see it forwarded here last week. He has not been prompt, as I would have desired, but I am sure our Heavenly Father will send the chair. Mrs. Muller is very sick on the sea, and has particularly desired to have this same chair, and not finding it here yesterday, we have made special prayer that our Heavenly Father would be pleased to provide it for us, and we will trust Him to do so.' As this dear man of God went peacefully on board, running the risk of Mrs. Muller making the trip without a chair, when, for a couple of dollars, she could have been provided for, I confess I feared Mr. Muller was carrying his faith principles too far and not acting wisely. I was kept at the express office ten minutes after Mr. Muller left. Just as I started to hurry to the wharf, a team drove up the street, and on top of a load just arrived from New York was *Mr. Muller's chair.* It was sent at once to the tender and placed in *my hands* to take to Mr. Muller, just as the boat was leaving the dock (the Lord having a lesson for me). Mr. Muller took it with the happy, pleased expression of a child who has just received a kindness deeply appreciated, and reverently removing his hat and folding his hands over it, he thanked the Heavenly Father for sending the chair.''

One of Melancthon's correspondents writes of Luther's praying: "I cannot enough admire the extraordinary, cheerfulness, constancy, faith and hope of the man in these trying and vexatious times. He constantly feeds these gracious affections by a very diligent study of the Word of God. *Then not a day passes in which he does not employ in prayer at least three of his very best hours.* Once I happened to hear him at prayer. Gracious God! What spirit and what faith is there in his expressions! He petitions God with as much reverence as if he was in the divine presence, and yet with as firm a hope and confidence as he would address a father or a friend.

'I know,' said he, 'Thou art our Father and our God; and therefore I am sure Thou wilt bring to naught the persecutors of Thy children. For shouldest Thou fail to do this Thine own cause, being connected with ours, would be endangered. It is entirely thine own concern. We, by Thy providence, have been compelled to take a part. Thou therefore wilt be our defence.' Whilst I was listening to Luther praying in this manner, at a distance, my soul seemed on fire within me, to hear the man address God so like a friend, yet with so much gravity and reverence; and also to hear him, in the course of his prayer, insisting on the promises contained in the Psalms, as if he were sure his petitions would be granted.''

Of William Bramwell, a noted Methodist preacher in England, wonderful for his zeal and prayer, the following is related by a sergeant major: ''In July, 1811, our regiment was ordered for Spain, then the seat of a protracted and sanguinary war. My mind was painfully exercised with the thoughts of leaving my dear wife and four helpless children in a strange country, unprotected and unprovided for. Mr. Bramwell felt a lively interest in our situation, and his sympathising spirit seemed to drink in all the agonised feelings of my tender wife. He supplicated the throne of grace day and night in our behalf. My wife and I spent the evening previous to our march at a friend's house, in company with Mr. Bramwell, who sat in a very pensive mood, and appeared to be in a spiritual struggle all the time. After supper, he suddenly pulled his hand out of his bosom, laid it on my knee, and said: 'Brother Riley, mark what I am about to say! You are not to go to Spain. Remember what I tell you, you are not; for I have been wrestling with God on your behalf, and when my Heavenly Father condescends in mercy to bless me with power to lay hold on

Himself, I do not easily let Him go; no, not until I am favoured with an answer. Therefore you may depend upon it that the next time I hear from you, you will be settled in quarters.' This came to pass exactly as he said. The next day the order for going to Spain was countermanded.''

These men prayed with a purpose. To them God was not far away, in some inaccessible region, but near at hand, ever ready to listen to the call of His children. There was no barrier between. They were on terms of perfect intimacy, if one may use such a phrase in relation to man and his Maker. No cloud obscured the face of the Father from His trusting child, who could look up into the Divine countenance and pour out the longings of his heart. And that is the type of prayer which God never fails to hear. He knows that it comes from a heart at one with His own; from one who is entirely yielded to the heavenly plan, and so He bends His ear and gives to the pleading child the assurance that his petition has been heard and answered.

Have we not all had some such experience when with set and undeviating purpose we have approached the face of our Father? In an agony of soul we have sought refuge from the oppression of the world in the anteroom of heaven; the waves of despair seemed to threaten destruction, and as no way of escape was visible anywhere, we fell back, like the disciples of old, upon the power of our Lord, crying to Him to save us lest we perish. And then in the twinkling of an eye, the thing was done. The billows sank into a calm; the howling wind died down at the Divine command; the agony of the soul passed into a restful peace as over the whole being there crept the consciousness of the Divine presence, bringing with it the assurance of answered prayer and sweet deliverance.

''I tell the Lord my troubles and difficulties, and wait

for Him to give me the answers to them," says one man of God. "And it is wonderful how a matter that looked very dark will in prayer become clear as crystal by the help of God's Spirit. I think Christians fail so often to get answers to their prayers because they do not wait long enough on God. They just drop down and say a few words, and then jump up and forget it and expect God to answer them. Such praying always reminds me of the small boy ringing his neighbour's door-bell, and then running away as fast as he can go."

When we acquire the habit of prayer we enter into a new atmosphere. "Do you expect to go to heaven?" asked someone of a devout Scotsman. "Why, man, I live there," was the quaint and unexpected reply. It was a pithy statement of a great truth, for all the way to heaven is heaven begun to the Christian who walks near enough to God to hear the secrets He has to impart.

This attitude is beautifully illustrated in a story of Horace Bushnell, told by Dr. Parkes Cadman. Bushnell was found to be suffering from an incurable disease. One evening the Rev. Joseph Twichell visited him, and, as they sat together under the starry sky, Bushnell said: "One of us ought to pray." Twichell asked Bushnell to do so, and Bushnell began his prayer; burying his face in the earth, he poured out his heart until, said Twichell, in recalling the incident, "I was afraid to stretch out my hand in the darkness lest I should touch God."

To have God thus near is to enter the holy of holies — to breathe the fragrance of the heavenly air, to walk in Eden's delightful gardens. Nothing but prayer can bring God and man into this happy communion. That was the experience of Samuel Rutherford, just as it is the experience of every one who passes through the same gateway. When this saint of God was confined in jail at one time for conscience sake, he enjoyed in a rare degree the Divine companionship, recording in his diary that Jesus entered his cell, and that at His coming "every stone flashed like a ruby."

Many others have borne witness to the same sweet fellowship, when prayer had become the one habit of life that meant more than anything else to them. David Livingstone lived in the realm of prayer and knew its gracious influence. It was his habit every birthday to write a prayer, and on the next to the last birthday of all, this was his prayer: "O Divine one, I have not loved Thee earnestly, deeply, sincerely enough. Grant, I pray Thee, that before this year is ended I may have finished my task." It was just on the threshold of the year that followed that his faithful men, as they looked into the hut of Ilala, while the rain dripped from the eaves, saw their master on his knees beside his bed in an attitude of prayer. He had died on his knees in prayer.

Stonewall Jackson was a man of prayer. Said he: "I have so fixed the habit in my mind that I never raise a glass of water to my lips without asking God's blessing, never seal a letter without putting a word of prayer under the seal, never take a letter from the post without a brief sending of my thoughts heavenward, never change my classes in the lecture-room without a minute's petition for the cadets who go out and for those who come in."

James Gilmour, the pioneer missionary to Mongolia, was a man of prayer. He had a habit in his writing of never using a blotter. He made a rule when he got to the bottom of any page to wait until the ink dried and spend the time in prayer.

In this way their whole being was saturated with the Divine, and they became the reflection of the heavenly fragrance and glory. Walking with God down the avenues of prayer we acquire something of His likeness, and unconsciously we become witnesses to others of His beauty and His grace. Professor James, in his famous work, "Varieties of Religious Experience," tells of a man of forty-nine who said: "God is more real to me than any thought or thing or person. I feel His presence positively, and the more as I live in closer harmony with His laws as written in my body and mind. I feel Him in the sunshine or rain; and all mingled with a delicious restfulness most nearly describes my feelings. I talk to Him as to a companion in prayer and praise, and our communion is delightful. He answers me again and again, often in words so clearly spoken that it seems my outer ear must have carried the tone, but generally in strong mental impressions. Usually a text of Scripture, unfolding some new view of Him and His love for me, and care for my safety ... That He is mine and I am His never leaves me; it is an abiding joy. Without it life would be a blank, a desert, a shoreless, trackless waste."

Equally notable is the testimony of Sir Thomas Browne, the beloved physician who lived at Norwich in 1605, and was the author of a very remarkable book of wide circulation, "Religio Medici." In spite of the fact that England was passing through a period of national convulsion and political excitement, he found comfort and strength in prayer. "I have resolved," he wrote in a journal found among his private papers after his death, "to pray more and pray always, to pray in all places where quietness inviteth, in the house, on the highway and on the street; and to know no street or passage in this city that may not witness that I have not forgotten God." And he adds: "I purpose to take occasion of praying upon the sight of any church which I may pass, that God may be worshipped there in spirit, and that souls may be saved there; to pray daily for my sick patients and for the patients of other physicians; at my entrance into any home to say, 'May the peace of God abide here'; after hearing a sermon, to pray for a blessing on God's truth, and upon the messenger; upon the sight of a beautiful person to bless God for His creatures, to pray for the beauty of such an one's soul, that God may enrich her with inward graces, and that the outward and inward may correspond; upon the sight of a deformed person, to pray God to give them wholeness of soul, and by and by to give them the beauty of the resurrection.''

What an illustration of the praying spirit! Such an attitude represents prayer without ceasing, reveals the habit of prayer in its unceasing supplication, in its uninterrupted communion, in its constant intercession. What an illustration, too, of purpose in prayer! Of how many of us can it be said that as we pass people in the street we pray for them, or that as we enter a home or a church we remember the inmates or the congregation in prayer to God?

The explanation of our thoughtlessness or forgetfulness lies in the fact that prayer with so many of us is simply a form of selfishness; it means asking for something for ourselves — that and nothing more.

And from such an attitude we need to pray to be delivered.

V

The prayer of faith is the only power in the universe to which the great Jehovah yields. Prayer is the sovereign remedy.—Robert Hall

The Church, intent on the acquisition of temporal power, had well nigh abandoned its spiritual duties, and its empire, which rested on spiritual foundations, was crumbling with their decay, and threatened to pass away like an unsubstantial vision.—Lea's Inquisition

Are we praying as Christ did? Do we abide in Him? Are our pleas and spirit the overflow of His spirit and pleas? Does love rule the spirit — perfect love?

These questions must be considered as proper and apposite at a time like the present. We do fear that we are doing more of other things than prayer. This is not a praying age; it is an age of great activity, of great movements, but one in which the tendency is very strong

37

to stress the seen and the material and to neglect and discount the unseen and the spiritual. Prayer is the greatest of all forces, because it honors God and brings Him into active aid.

There can be no substitute, no rival for prayer; it stands alone as the great spiritual force, and this force must be imminent and acting. It cannot be dispensed with during one generation, nor held in abeyance for the advance of any great movement — it must be continuous and particular, always, everywhere, and in everything. We cannot run our spiritual operations on the prayers of the past generation. Many persons believe in the efficacy of prayer, but not many pray. Prayer is the easiest and hardest of all things; the simplest and the sublimest; the weakest and the most powerful; its results lie outside the range of human possibilities — they are limited only by the omnipotence of God.

Few Christians have anything but a vague idea of the power of prayer; fewer still have any experience of that power. The Church seems almost wholly unaware of the power God puts into her hand; this spiritual *carte blanche* on the infinite resources of God's wisdom and power is rarely, if ever, used — never used to the full measure of honouring God. It is astounding how poor the use, how little the benefits. Prayer is our most formidable weapon, but the one in which we are the least skilled, the most averse to its use. We do everything else for the heathen save the thing God wants us to do; the only thing which does any good — makes all else we do efficient.

To graduate in the school of prayer is to master the whole course of a religious life. The first and last stages of holy living are crowned with praying. It is a life trade. The hindrances of prayer are the hindrances in a holy life. The conditions of praying are the conditions of righteousness, holiness and salvation. A cobbler in the trade of praying is a bungler in the trade of salvation.

Prayer is a trade to be learned. We must be apprentices and serve our time at it. Painstaking care, much thought, practice and labour are required to be a skillful tradesman in praying. Practice in this, as well as in all other trades, makes perfect. Toiling hands and hearts only make proficients in this heavenly trade.

In spite of the benefits and blessings which flow from communion with God, the sad confession must be made that we are not praying much. A very small number comparatively lead in prayer at the meetings. Fewer still pray in their families. Fewer still are in the habit of praying regularly in their closets. Meetings specially for prayer are as rare as frost in June. In many churches there is neither the name nor the semblance of a prayer meeting. In the town and city churches the prayer meeting in name is not a prayer meeting in fact. A sermon or a lecture is the main feature. Prayer is the nominal attachment.

Our people are not essentially a praying people. That is evident by their lives.

Prayer and a holy life are one. They mutually act and react. Neither can survive alone. The absence of the one is the absence of the other. The monk depraved prayer, substituted superstition for praying, mummeries and routine for a holy life. We are in danger of substituting churchly work and a ceaseless round of showy activities for prayer and holy living. A holy life does not live in the closet, but it cannot live without the closet. If, by any chance, a prayer chamber should be established without a holy life, it would be a chamber without the presence of God in it.

Put the saints everywhere to praying, is the burden of the apostolic effort and the key note of apostolic success.

Jesus Christ had striven to do this in the days of His personal ministry. He was moved by infinite compassion at the ripened fields of earth perishing for lack of labourers, and pausing in His own praying, He tries to awaken the sleeping sensibilities of His disciples to the duty of prayer, as He charges them: "Pray ye the Lord of the harvest that He will send forth labourers into His harvest." And He spake a parable to them to this end, that *men ought* always to pray.

Only glimpses of this great importance of prayer could the apostles get before Pentecost. But the Spirit coming and filling on Pentecost elevated prayer to its vital and all-commanding position in the Gospel of Christ. The call now of prayer to every saint is the Spirit's loudest and most exigent call. Sainthood's piety is made, refined, perfected, by prayer. The Gospel moves with slow and timid pace when the saints are not at their prayers early and late and long.

Where are the Christlike leaders who can teach the modern saints how to pray and put them at it? Do our leaders know we are raising up a prayerless set of saints? Where are the apostolic leaders who can put God's people to praying? Let them come to the front and do the work, and it will be the greatest work that can be done. An increase of educational facilities and a great increase of money force will be the direst curse to religion if they are not sanctified by more and better praying than we are doing.

More praying will not come as a matter of course. The campaign for the twentieth or thirtieth century will not help our praying, but hinder if we are not careful. Nothing but a specific effort from a praying leadership will avail. None but praying leaders can have praying followers. Praying apostles will beget praying saints. A praying pulpit will beget praying pews. We do greatly need somebody who can set the saints to this business of praying. We are a generation of non-praying saints. Non-praying saints are a beggarly gang of saints, who have neither the ardour nor the beauty, nor the power of saints. Who will restore this branch? The greatest will he be of reformers and apostles, who can set the Church to praying.

Holy men have, in the past, changed the whole force of affairs, revolutionised character and country by prayer. And such achievements are still possible to us. The power is only wanting to be used. Prayer is but the expression of faith.

Time would fail to tell of the mighty things wrought by prayer, for by it holy ones have "subdued kingdoms, wrought righteousness, obtained promises, stopped the mouths of lions, quenched the violence of fire, escaped the edge of the sword, out of weakness were made strong, waxed valiant in fight, turned to fight the armies of the aliens, women received their dead raised to life again."

Prayer honours God; it dishonours self. It is man's plea of weakness, ignorance, want. A plea which heaven cannot disregard. God delights to have us pray.

Prayer is not the foe to work, it does not paralyse activity. It works mightily; prayer itself is the greatest work. It springs activity, stimulates desire and effort. Prayer is not an opiate but a tonic, it does not lull to sleep but arouses anew for action. The lazy man does not, will not, cannot pray, for prayer demands energy. Paul calls it a striving, an agony. With Jacob it was a wrestling; with the Syrophenician women it was a struggle which called into play all the higher qualities of the soul, and which demanded great force to meet.

The closet is not an asylum for the indolent and worthless Christian. It is not a nursery where none but babes belong. It is the battlefield of the Church; its citadel; the scene of heroic and unearthly conflicts. The closet is the base of supplies for the Christian and the Church. Cut off from it there is nothing left but retreat and disaster. The energy for work, the mastery over self, the deliverance from fear, all spiritual results and graces, are much advanced by prayer. The difference between the strength, the experience, the holiness of Christians is found in the contrast in their praying.

Few, short, feeble prayers, always betoken a low spiritual condition. Men ought to pray much and apply themselves to it with energy and perseverance. Eminent Christians have been eminent in prayer. The deep things of God are learned nowhere else. Great things for God are done by great prayers. He who prays much, studies much, loves much, works much, does much for God and humanity. The execution of the Gospel, the vigour of faith, the maturity and excellence of spiritual graces wait on prayer.

VI

"Nothing is impossible to industry," said one of the seven sages of Greece. Let us change the word industry for persevering prayer, and the motto will be more Christian and more worthy of universal adoption. I am persuaded that we are all more deficient in a spirit of prayer than in any other grace. God loves importunate prayer so much that He will not give us much blessing without it. And the reason that He loves such prayer is that He loves us and knows that it is a necessary preparation for our receiving the richest blessings which He is waiting and longing to bestow.

I never prayed sincerely and earnestly for anything but it came at some time — no matter at how distant a day, somehow, in some shape, probably the last I would have devised, it came.—Adoniram Judson

It is good, I find, to persevere in attempts to pray. If I cannot pray with perseverance or continue long in my address to the Divine Being, I have found

that the more I do in secret prayer the more I have delight to do, and have enjoyed more of the spirit of prayer; and frequently I have found the contrary, when by journeying or otherwise, I have been deprived of retirement.—David Brainerd

Christ puts importunity as a distinguishing characteristic of true praying. We must not only pray, but we must pray with great urgency, with intentness and with repetition. We must not only pray, but we must pray again and again. We must not get tired of praying. We must be thoroughly in earnest, deeply concerned about the things for which we ask, for Jesus Christ made it very plain that the secret of prayer and its success lie in its urgency. We must press our prayers upon God.

In a parable of exquisite pathos and simplicity, our Lord taught not simply that men ought to pray, but that men ought to pray with full heartiness, and press the matter with vigorous energy and brave hearts.

"And He spake a parable unto them to the end that they ought always to pray, and not to faint; saying, There was in a city, a judge, which feared not God, and regarded not man: and there was a widow in that city; and she came oft unto him, saying, Avenge me of mine adversary. And he would not for a while: but afterwards he said within himself, Though I fear not God, nor regard man; yet because this widow troubleth me, I will avenge her, lest she wear me out by her continual coming. And the Lord said, Hear what the unrighteous judge saith. And shall not God avenge His elect, which cry to Him day and night, and He is longsuffering over them? I say unto you, that He will avenge them speedily. Howbeit when the Son of man cometh, shall He find faith on the earth?"

This poor woman's case was a most hopeless one, but importunity brings hope from the realms of despair and creates success where neither success nor its conditions existed. There could be no stronger case, to show how unwearied and dauntless importunity gains its ends where everything else fails. The preface to this parable says: "He spake a parable to this end, that men ought always to pray and not to faint." He knew that men would soon get faint-hearted in praying, so to hearten us He gives this picture of the marvellous power of importunity.

The widow, weak and helpless, is helplessness personified; bereft of every hope and influence which could move an unjust judge, she yet wins her case solely by her tireless and offensive importunity. Could the necessity of importunity, its power and tremendous importance in prayer, be pictured in deeper or more impressive colouring? It surmounts or removes all obstacles, overcomes every resisting force and gains its ends in the face of invincible hindrances. We can do nothing without prayer. All things can be done by importunate prayer.

That is the teaching of Jesus Christ.

Another parable spoken by Jesus enforces the same great truth. A man at midnight goes to his friend for a loan of bread. His pleas are strong, based on friendship and the embarrassing and exacting demands of necessity, but these all fail. He gets no bread, but he stays and presses, and waits and gains. Sheer importunity succeeds where all other pleas and influences had failed.

The case of the Syrophenician woman is a parable in action. She is arrested in her approaches to Christ by the information that He will not see anyone. She is denied His presence, and then in His presence is treated with seeming indifference, with the chill of silence and unconcern: she presses and approaches, the pressure and approach are repulsed by the stern and crushing statement that He is not sent to her kith or kind, that she is reprobated from His mission and power. She is humiliated by being called a dog. Yet she accepts all, overcomes all, wins all by her humble, dauntless, invincible importunity. The Son of God, pleased, surprised, overpowered by her unconquerable importunity, says to her: "O, woman, great is thy faith; be it unto thee even as thou wilt." Jesus Christ surrenders Himself to the importunity of a great faith. "And shall not God avenge His own elect which cry day and night unto Him, though He bear long with them?"

Jesus Christ puts ability to importune as one of the elements of prayer, one of the main conditions of prayer. The prayer of the Syrophenician woman is an exhibition of the matchless power of importunity, of a conflict more real and involving more of vital energy, endurance, and all the higher elements than was ever illustrated in the conflicts of Isthmia or Olympia.

The first lessons of importunity are taught in the Sermon on the Mount — "Ask, and it shall be given; seek, and ye shall find; knock, and it shall be opened." These are steps of advance — "For every one that asketh, receiveth; and he that seeketh, findeth; and to him that knocketh, it shall be opened."

Without continuance the prayer may go unanswered. Importunity is made up of the ability to hold on, to press on, to wait with unrelaxed and unrelaxable grasp, restless desire and restful patience. Importunate prayer is not an incident, but the main thing, not a performance but a passion, not a need but a necessity.

Prayer in its highest form and grandest success assumes the attitude of a wrestler with God. It is the contest, trial and victory of faith; a victory not secured from an enemy, but from Him who tries our faith that

He may enlarge it: that tests our strength to make us stronger. Few things give such quickened and permanent vigour to the soul as a long exhaustive season of importunate prayer. It makes an experience, an epoch, a new calendar for the spirit, a new life to religion, a soldierly training. The Bible never wearies in its pressure and illustration of the fact that the highest spiritual good is secured as the return of the outgoing of the highest form of spiritual effort. There is neither encouragement nor room in Bible religion for feeble desires, listless efforts, lazy attitudes; all must be strenuous, urgent, ardent. Inflamed desires, impassioned, unwearied insistence delight heaven. God would have His children incorrigibly in earnest and persistently bold in their efforts. Heaven is too busy to listen to half-hearted prayers or to respond to pop-calls.

Our whole being must be in our praying; like John Knox, we must say and feel, "Give me Scotland, or I die." Our experience and revelations of God are born of our costly sacrifice, our costly conflicts, our costly praying. The wrestling, all night praying, of Jacob made an era never to be forgotten in Jacob's life, brought God to the rescue, changed Esau's attitude and conduct, changed Jacob's character, saved and affected his life and entered into the habits of a nation.

Our seasons of importunate prayer cut themselves like the print of a diamond, into our hardest places, and mark with ineffaceable traces our characters. They are the salient periods of our lives! The memorial stones which endure and to which we turn.

Importunity, it may be repeated, is a condition of prayer. We are to press the matter, not with vain repetitions, but with urgent repetitions. We repeat, not to count the times, but to gain the prayer. We cannot quit praying because heart and soul are in it. We pray "with

47

all perseverance." We hang to our prayers because by them we live. We press our pleas because we must have them or die. Christ gives us two most expressive parables to emphasise the necessity of importunity in praying. Perhaps Abraham lost Sodom by failing to press to the utmost his privilege of praying. Joash, we know, lost because he stayed his smiting.

Perseverance counts much with God as well as with man. If Elijah had ceased at his first petition the heavens would have scarcely yielded their rain to his feeble praying. If Jacob had quit praying at decent bedtime he would scarcely have survived the next day's meeting with Esau. If the Syrophenician woman had allowed her faith to faint by silence, humiliation, repulse, or stop mid-way its struggles, her grief-stricken home would never have been brightened by the healing of her daughter.

Pray and never faint, is the motto Christ gives us for praying. It is the test of our faith, and the severer the trial and the longer the waiting, the more glorious the results.

The benefits and necessity of importunity are taught by Old Testament saints. Praying men must be strong in hope, and faith, and prayer. They must know how to wait and to press, to wait on God and be in earnest in our approaches to Him.

Abraham has left us an example of importunate intercession in his passionate pleading with God on behalf of Sodom and Gomorrah, and if, as already indicated, he had not ceased in his asking, perhaps God would not have ceased in His giving.

"Abraham left off asking before God left off granting." Moses taught the power of importunity when he interceded for Israel forty days and forty nights, by fasting and prayer. And he succeeded in his importunity.

Jesus, in His teaching and example, illustrated and perfected this principle of Old Testament pleading and waiting. How strange that the only Son of God, who came on a mission direct from His Father, whose only heaven on earth, whose only life and law were to do His Father's will in that mission — what a mystery that He should be under the law of prayer, that the blessings which came to Him were impregnated and purchased by prayer; stranger still that importunity in prayer was the process by which His wealthiest supplies from God were gained. Had He not prayed with importunity, no transfiguration would have been in His history, no mighty works had rendered Divine His career. His all-night praying was that which filled with compassion and power His all-day work. The importunate praying of His life crowned His death with its triumph. He learned the high lesson of submission to God's will in the struggles of importunate prayer before He illustrated that submission so sublimely on the cross.

"Whether we like it or not," said Mr. Spurgeon, *"asking is the rule of the kingdom."* 'Ask, and ye shall receive.' It is a rule that never will be altered in anybody's case. Our Lord Jesus Christ is the elder brother of the family, but God has not relaxed the rule for Him. Remember this text: Jehovah says to His own Son, 'Ask of Me, and I will give Thee the heaven for Thine inheritance, and the uttermost parts of the earth for Thy possession.' If the Royal and Divine Son of God cannot be exempted from the rule of asking that He may have, you and I cannot expect the rule to be relaxed in our favour. Why should it be? What reason can be pleaded why we should be exempted from prayer? What argument can there be why we should be deprived of the privilege and delivered from the necessity of supplication? I can see none: can you? God will bless Elijah and send rain on

Israel, but Elijah must pray for it. If the chosen nation is to prosper, Samuel must plead for it. If the Jews are to be delivered, Daniel must intercede. God will bless Paul, and the nations shall be converted through him, but Paul must pray. Pray he did without ceasing; his epistles show that he expected nothing except by asking for it. If you may have everything by asking, and nothing without asking, I beg you to see how absolutely vital prayer is, and I beseech you to abound in it.''

There is not the least doubt that much of our praying fails for lack of persistency. It is without the fire and strength of perseverance. Persistence is of the essence of true praying. It may not be always called into exercise, but it must be there as the reserve force. Jesus taught that perseverance is the essential element of prayer. Men must be in earnest when they kneel at God's footstool.

Too often we get faint-hearted and quit praying at the point where we ought to begin. We let go at the very point where we should hold on strongest. Our prayers are weak because they are not impassioned by an unfailing and resistless will.

God loves the importunate pleader, and sends him answers that would never have been granted but for the persistency that refuses to let go until the petition craved for is granted.

VII

I suspect I have been allotting habitually too little time to religious exercises as private devotion, religious meditation, Scripture reading, etc. Hence I am lean and cold and hard. God would perhaps prosper me more in spiritual things if I were to be more diligent in using the means of grace. I had better allot more time, say two hours or an hour and a half, to religious exercises daily, and try whether by so doing I cannot preserve a frame of spirit more habitually devotional, a more lively sense of unseen things, a warmer love to God, and a greater degree of hunger and thirst after righteousness, a heart less prone to be soiled with worldly cares, designs, passions, and apprehension and a real undissembled longing for heaven, its pleasures and its purity.—William Wilberforce

"Men ought *always* to pray, and not to faint." The words are the words of our Lord, who not only ever sought to impress upon His followers the urgency and the importance of prayer, but set them an example which they alas! have been far too slow to copy.

The *always* speaks for itself. Prayer is not a meaningless function or duty to be crowded into the busy or the weary ends of the day, and we are not obeying our Lord's command when we content ourselves with a few minutes upon our knees in the morning rush or late at night when the faculties, tired with the tasks of the day, call out for rest. God is always within call, it is true; His ear is ever attentive to the cry of His child, but we can never get to know Him if we use the vehicle of prayer as we use the telephone — for a few words of hurried conversation. Intimacy requires development. We can never know God as it is our privilege to know Him, by brief and fragmentary and unconsidered repetitions of intercessions that are requests for personal favours and nothing more. That is not the way in which we can come into communication with heaven's King. "The goal of prayer is the ear of God," a goal that can only be reached by patient and continued and continuous waiting upon Him, pouring out our heart to Him and permitting Him to speak to us. Only by so doing can we expect to know Him, and as we come to know Him better we shall spend more time in His presence and find that presence a constant and ever-increasing delight.

Always does not mean that we are to neglect the ordinary duties of life; what it means is that the soul which has come into intimate contact with God in the silence of the prayer-chamber is never out of conscious touch with the Father, that the heart is always going out to Him in loving communion, and that the moment the mind is released from the task upon which it is engaged it returns as naturally to God as the bird does to its nest. What a beautiful conception of prayer we get if we regard it in this light, if we view it as a constant fellowship, an unbroken audience with the King. Prayer then loses every vestige of dread which it may once have possessed; we regard it no longer as a duty which must be performed, but rather as a privilege which is to be enjoyed, a rare delight that is always revealing some new beauty.

Thus, when we open our eyes in the morning, our thought instantly mounts heavenward. To many Christians the morning hours are the most precious portion of the day, because they provide the opportunity for the hallowed fellowship that gives the keynote to the day's programme. And what better introduction can there be to the never-ceasing glory and wonder of a new day than to spend it alone with God? It is said that Mr. Moody, at a time when no other place was available, kept his morning watch in the coal-shed, pouring out his heart to God, and finding in his precious Bible a true "feast of fat things."

George Muller also combined Bible study with prayer in the quiet morning hours. At one time his practice was to give himself to prayer, after having dressed, in the morning. Then his plan underwent a change. As he himself put it: "I saw the most important thing I had to do was to give myself to the reading of the Word of God, and to meditation on it, that thus my heart might be comforted, encouraged, warned, reproved, instructed; and that thus, by means of the Word of God, whilst meditating on it, my heart might be brought into experimental communion with the Lord. I began, therefore, to meditate on the New Testament early in the morning. The first thing I did, after having asked in a few words for the Lord's blessing upon his precious Word, was to begin to meditate on the Word of God, searching as it were, into every verse to get blessing out of it; not for the sake of the public ministry of the Word, not for the sake of preaching on what I had meditated on, but for the sake of obtaining food for my own soul. The result I have found to be almost invariably thus, that after a very few minutes my soul has been led to confession, or to thanksgiving, or to intercession, or to supplication; so that, though I did not, as it were, give myself to prayer, but to meditation, yet it turned almost immediately more or less into prayer."

The study of the Word and prayer go together, and where we find the one truly practised, the other is sure to be seen in close alliance.

But we do not pray *always*. That is the trouble with so many of us. We need to pray much more than we do and much longer than we do.

Robert Murray McCheyne, gifted and saintly, of whom it was said, that "Whether viewed as a son, a brother, a friend, or a pastor, he was the most faultless and attractive exhibition of the true Christian they had ever seen embodied in a living form," knew what it was to spend much time upon his knees, and he never wearied in urging upon others the joy and the value of holy intercession. "God's children should pray," he said. "They should cry day and night to Him, God hears every one of your cries in the busy hour of the daytime and in the lonely watches of the night." In every way, by preaching, by exhortation when present and by letters when absent, McCheyne emphasised the vital duty of prayer, importunate and unceasing prayer.

In his diary we find this: "In the morning was engaged in preparing the head, then the heart. This has been frequently my error, and I have always felt the evil of it, especially in prayer. Reform it then, O Lord." While on his trip to the Holy Land he wrote: "For much of our safety I feel indebted to the prayers of my people. If the veil of the world's machinery were lifted off how much we would find done in answer to the prayers of God's children.'' In an ordination sermon he said to the preacher: ''Give yourself to prayers and the ministry of the Word. If you do not pray, God will probably lay you aside from your ministry, as He did me, to teach you to pray. Remember Luther's maxim, 'To have prayed well is to have studied well.' Get your texts from God, your thoughts, your words. Carry the names of the little flock upon your breast like the High Priest. Wrestle for the unconverted. Luther spent his last three hours in prayer; John Welch prayed seven or eight hours a day. He used to keep a plaid on his bed that he might wrap himself in when he rose during the night. Sometimes his wife found him on the ground lying weeping. When she complained, he would say, 'O, woman, I have the souls of three thousand to answer for, and I know not how it is with many of them.''' The people he exhorted and charged: ''Pray for your pastor. Pray for his body, that he may be kept strong and spared many years. Pray for his soul, that he may be kept humble and holy, a burning and shining light. Pray for his ministry, that it may be abundantly blessed, that he may be anointed to preach good tidings. Let there be no secret prayer without naming him before your God, no family prayer without carrying your pastor in your hearts to God.''

''Two things,'' says his biographer, ''he seems never to have ceased from — the cultivation of personal holiness and the most anxious efforts to win souls.'' The two are the inseparable attendants on the ministry of prayer. Prayer fails when the desire and effort for personal holiness fail. No person is a soul-winner who is not an adept in the ministry of prayer. ''It is the duty of ministers,'' says this holy man, ''to begin the reformation of religion and manner with themselves, families, etc., with confession of past sin, earnest prayer for direction, grace and full purpose of heart." He begins with himself under the head of "Reformation in Secret Prayer," and he resolves:

"I ought not to omit any of the parts of prayer — confession, adoration, thanksgiving, petition and intercession. There is a fearful tendency to omit *confession* proceeding from low views of God and His law, slight views of my heart, and the sin of my past life. This must be resisted. There is a constant tendency to omit *adoration* when I forget to Whom I am speaking, when I rush heedlessly into the presence of Jehovah without thought of His awful name and character. When I have little eyesight for his glory, and little admiration of His wonders, I have the native tendency of the heart to omit giving *thanks,* and yet it is specially commanded. Often when the heart is dead to the salvation of others I omit *intercession,* and yet it especially is the spirit of the great Advocate Who has the name of Israel on His heart. I ought to pray before seeing anyone. Often when I sleep long, or meet with others early, and then have family prayer and breakfast and forenoon callers, it is eleven or twelve o'clock before I begin secret prayer. This is a wretched system; it is unscriptural. Christ rose before day and went into a solitary place. David says, 'Early will I seek Thee; Thou shalt early hear my voice.' Mary Magdalene came to the sepulchre while it was yet dark. Family prayer loses much of its power and sweetness; and I can do no good to those who come to seek from me. The conscience feels guilty, the soul unfed, the lamp not trimmed. I feel it is far better to begin with God, to see His face first, to get my soul near Him before it is near another. 'When I awake I am still with Thee.'" If I have slept too long, or I am going an early journey, or my time is in any way shortened, it is best to dress hurriedly and to have a few minutes alone with God than to give up all for lost. But in general it is best to have at least one hour alone with God before engaging in anything else. I ought to spend the best hours of the day in communion with God. When I awake in the night, I ought to rise and pray as David and John Welch.''

McCheyne believed in being *always* in prayer, and his fruitful life, short though that life was, affords an illustration of the power that comes from long and frequent visits to the secret place where we keep tryst with our Lord.

Men of McCheyne's stamp are needed today — praying men, who know how to give themselves to the greatest task demanding their time and their attention; men who can give their whole heart to the holy task of intercession, men who can pray through. God's cause is committed to men; God commits Himself to men. Praying men are the vicegerents of God; they do His work and carry out His plans.

We are obliged to pray if we be citizens of God's Kingdom. Prayerlessness is expatriation, or worse, from God's Kingdom. It is outlawry, a high crime, a constitutional breach. The Christian who relegates prayer to a subordinate place in his life soon loses whatever spiritual zeal he may have once possessed, and the Church that makes little of prayer cannot maintain vital piety, and is powerless to advance the Gospel. The Gospel cannot live, fight, conquer without prayer — prayer unceasing, instant and ardent.

Little prayer is the characteristic of a backslidden age and of a backslidden Church. Whenever there is little praying in the pulpit or in the pew, spiritual bankruptcy is imminent and inevitable.

The cause of God has no commercial age, no cultured age, no age of education, no age of money. But it has one golden age, and that is the age of prayer. When its leaders are men of prayer, when prayer is the prevailing element of worship, like the incense giving continual fragrance to its service, then the cause of God will be triumphant.

Better praying and more of it, that is what we need. We need holier men, and more of them, holier women, and more of them to pray — women like Hannah, who, out of their greatest griefs and temptations brewed their greatest prayers. Through prayer Hannah found her relief. Everywhere the Church was backslidden and apostate, her foes were victorious. Hannah gave herself to prayer, and in sorrow she multiplied her praying. She saw a great revival born of her praying. When the whole nation was oppressed, prophet and priest, Samuel was born to establish a new line of priesthood, and her praying warmed into life a new life for God. Everywhere religion revived and flourished. God, true to His promise, *"Ask of Me,"* though the praying came from a woman's broken heart, heard and answered, sending a new day of holy gladness to revive His people.

So once more, let us apply the emphasis and repeat that the great need of the Church in this and all ages is men of such commanding faith, of such unsullied holiness, of such marked spiritual vigour and consuming zeal, that they will work spiritual revolutions through their mighty praying. "Natural ability and educational advantages do not figure as factors in this matter; but a capacity for faith, the ability to pray, the power of a thorough consecration, the ability of self-littleness, an absolute losing of one's self in God's glory and an ever present and insatiable yearning and seeking after all the fulness of God. Men who can set the Church ablaze for God, not in a noisy, showy way, but with an intense and quiet heat that melts and moves every thing for God."

And, to return to the vital point, secret praying is the test, the gauge, the conserver of man's relation to God. The prayer-chamber, while it is the test of the sincerity of our devotion to God, becomes also the measure of the devotion. The self-denial, the sacrifices which we make for our prayer-chambers, the frequency of our visits to that hallowed place of meeting with the Lord, the lingering to stay, the loathness to leave, are values which we put on communion alone with God, the price we pay for the Spirit's trysting hours of heavenly love.

The prayer-chamber conserves our relation to God. It hems every raw edge; it tucks up every flowing and entangling garment; girds up every fainting loin. The sheet-anchor holds not the ship more surely and safely than the prayer-chamber holds to God. Satan has to break our hold on, and close up our way to the prayer-chambers, ere he can break our hold on God or close up our way to heaven.

> "Be not afraid to pray; to pray is right;
>   Pray if thou canst with hope, but ever pray,
> Though hope be weak or sick with long delay;
>   Pray in the darkness if there be no light;
> And if for any wish thou dare not pray
>   Then pray to God to cast that wish away."

VIII

In God's name I beseech you let prayer nourish your soul as your meals nourish your body. Let your fixed seasons of prayer keep you in God's presence through the day, and His presence frequently remembered through it be an ever-fresh spring of prayer. Such a brief, loving recollection of God renews a man's whole being, quiets his passions, supplies light and counsel in difficulty, gradually subdues the temper, and causes him to possess his soul in patience, or rather gives it up to the possession of God.—Fenelon

Devoted too much time and attention to outward and public duties of the ministry. But this has a mistaken conduct, for I have learned that neglect of much and fervent communion with God in meditation and prayer is not the way to redeem the time nor to fit me for public ministrations.

I rightly attribute my present deadness to want of sufficient time and tranquillity for private devotion.

Want of more reading, retirement and private devotion, I have little mastery over my own tempers. An unhappy day to me for want of more solitude and prayer. If there be anything I do, if there be anything I leave undone, let me be perfect in prayer.

After all, whatever God may appoint, prayer is the great thing. Oh that I may be a man of prayer.

—Henry Martyn

That the men had quit praying in Paul's time we cannot certainly affirm. They have, in the main, quit praying now. They are too busy to pray. Time and strength and every faculty are laid under tribute to money, to business, to the affairs of the world. Few men lay themselves out in great praying. The great business of praying is a hurried, petty, starved, beggarly business with most men.

St. Paul calls a halt, and lays a levy on men for prayer. Put the men to praying is Paul's unfailing remedy for great evils in Church, in State, in politics, in business, in home. Put the men to praying, then politics will be cleansed, business will be thriftier, the Church will be holier, the home will be sweeter.

"I exhort, therefore, first of all, that supplications, prayers, intercessions, thanksgivings, be made for all men; for kings and all that are in high place; that we may lead a tranquil and quiet life in all godliness and gravity. This is good and acceptable in the sight of God our Saviour ... I desire, therefore, that the men pray in every place, lifting up holy hands, without wrath and disputing (I Timothy ii. 1-3, 8).

Praying women and children are invaluable to God, but if their praying is not supplemented by praying men, there will be a great loss in the power of prayer — a great breach and depreciation in the value of prayer, great paralysis in the energy of the Gospel. Jesus Christ spake a parable unto the people, telling them that men ought always to pray and not faint. Men who are strong in everything else ought to be strong in prayer, and never yield to discouragement, weakness or depression. Men who are brave, persistent, redoubtable in other pursuits ought to be full of courage, unfainting, strong-hearted in prayer.

Men are to pray; *all men* are to pray. Men, as distinguished from women, men in their strength in their wisdom. There is an absolute, specific command that the men pray; there is an absolute imperative necessity that men pray. The first of beings, man, should also be first in prayer.

The men are to pray for men. The direction is specific and classified. Just underneath we have a specific direction with regard to women. About prayer, its importance, wideness and practice the Bible here deals with the men in contrast to, and distinct from, the women. The men are definitely commanded, seriously charged, and warmly exhorted to pray. Perhaps it was that men were averse to prayer, or indifferent to it; it may be that they deemed it a small thing, and gave to it neither time nor value nor significance. But God would have all men pray, and so the great Apostle lifts the subject into prominence and emphases its importance.

For prayer is of transcendent importance. Prayer is the mightiest agent to advance God's work. Praying hearts and hands only can do God's work. Prayer succeeds when all else fails. Prayer has won great victories, and rescued, with notable triumph, God's saints when every other hope was gone. Men who know how to pray are the greatest boon God can give to earth — they are the richest gift earth can offer heaven. Men who know how to use this weapon of prayer are God's best soldiers. His mightiest leaders.

Praying men are God's chosen leaders. The distinction between the leaders that God brings to the front to lead and bless His people, and those leaders who owe their position of leadership to a worldly, selfish, unsanctified selection, is this, God's leaders are pre-eminently men of prayer. This distinguishes them as the simple, Divine attestation of their call, the seal of their separation by God. Whatever of other graces or gifts they may have, the gift and grace of prayer towers above them all. In whatever else they may share or differ, in the gift of prayer, they are one.

What would God's leaders be without prayer? Strip Moses of his power in prayer, a gift that made him eminent in pagan estimate, and the crown is taken from his head, the food and fire of his faith are gone. Elijah, without his praying, would have neither record nor place in the Divine legation, his life insipid, cowardly, its energy, defiance and fire gone. Without Elijah's praying the Jordan would never have yielded to the stroke of his mantle, nor would the stern angel of death have honored him with the chariot and horses of fire. The argument that God used to quiet the fears and convince Ananias of Paul's condition and sincerity is the epitome of his history, the solution of his life and work — "Behold he prayeth."

Paul, Luther, Wesley — what would these chosen ones of God be without the distinguishing and controlling element of prayer? They were leaders for God because mighty in prayer. They were not leaders because of brilliancy in thought, because exhaustless in resources, because of their magnificent culture or native endowment, but leaders because by the power of prayer they could command the power of God. Praying men means much more than men who say prayers; much more than men who pray by habit. It means men with whom prayer is a mighty force, an energy that moves heaven and pours untold treasures of good on earth.

Praying men are the safety of the Church from the materialism that is affecting all its plans and polity, and which is hardening the life-blood. The insinuation circulates as a secret, deadly poison that the Church is not so dependent on purely spiritual forces as it used to be — that changed times and changed conditions have brought it out of its spiritual straits and dependencies and put it where other forces can bear it to its climax. A fatal snare of this kind has allured the Church into worldly embraces, dazzled her leaders, weakened her foundations, and shorn her of much of her beauty and strength. Praying men are the saviours of the Church from this material tendency. They pour into it the original spiritual forces, lift it off the sand-bars of materialism, and press it out into the ocean depths of spiritual power. Praying men keep God in the Church in full force; keep His hand on the helm, and train the Church in its lessons of strength and trust.

The number and efficiency of the labourers in God's vineyard in all lands is dependent on the men of prayer. The mightiness of these men of prayer increases, by the divinely arranged process, the number and success of the consecrated labours. Prayer opens wide their doors of access, gives holy aptness to enter, and holy boldness, firmness, and fruitage. Praying men are needed in all fields of spiritual labour. There is no position in the Church of God, high or low, which can be well filled without instant prayer. No position where Christians are found that does not demand the full play of a faith that always prays and never faints. Praying men are needed in the house of business, as well as in the house of God, that they may order and direct trade, not according to the maxims of this world, but according to Bible precepts and the maxims of the heavenly world.

Men of prayer are needed especially in the positions of Church influence, honour, and power. These leaders of Church thought, of Church work, and of Church life should be men of signal power in prayer. It is the praying heart that sanctifies the toil and skill of the hands, and the toil and wisdom of the head. Prayer keeps work in the line of God's will, and keeps thought in the line of God's Word. The solemn responsibilities of leadership, in a large or limited sphere, in God's Church should be so hedged about with prayer that between it and the world there should be an impassable gulf, so elevated and purified by prayer that neither cloud nor night should stain the radiance nor dim the sight of a constant meridian view of God. Many Church leaders seem to think if they can be prominent as men of business, of money, influence, of thought, of plans, of scholarly attainments, of eloquent gifts, of taking, conspicuous activities, that these are enough, and will atone for the absence of the higher spiritual power which much praying only can give. But how vain and paltry are these in the serious work of bringing glory to God, controlling the Church for Him, and bringing it into full accord with its Divine mission.

Praying men arc the men that have done so much for God in the past. They are the ones who have won the victories for God, and spoiled His foes. They are the ones who have set up His Kingdom in the very camps of His enemies. There are no other conditions of success in this day. The twentieth century has no relief statute to suspend the necessity or force of prayer — no substitute by which its gracious ends can be secured. We are shut up to this, praying hands only can build for God. They are God's mighty ones on earth, His master-builders. They may be destitute of all else, but with the wrestlings and prevailings of a simple-hearted faith they are mighty, the mighiest for God. Church leaders may be gifted in all else, but without this greatest of gifts they are as Samson shorn of his locks, or as the Temple without the Divine presence or the Divine glory, and on whose altars the heavenly flame has died.

The only protection and rescue from worldliness lie in our intense and radical spirituality; and our only hope for the existence and maintenance of this high, saving spirituality, under God, is in the purest and most aggressive leadership — a leadership that knows the secret power of prayer, the sign by which the Church has conquered, and that has conscience, conviction, and courage to hold true to her symbols, true to her traditions, and true to the hidings of her power. We need this prayerful leadership; we must have it, that by the perfection and beauty of its holiness, by the strength and elevation of its faith, by the potency and pressure of its prayers, by the authority and spotlessness of its example, by the fire and contagion of its zeal, by the singularity, sublimity, and unworldliness of its piety, it may influence God and hold and mould the Church to its heavenly pattern.

Such leaders, how mightily they are felt. How their flame arouses the Church! How they stir it by the force of their Pentecostal presence! How they embattle and give victory by the conflicts and triumphs of their own faith! How they fashion it by the impress and importunity of their prayers! How they inoculate it by the contagion and fire of their holiness! How they lead the march in great spiritual revolutions! How the Church is raised from the dead by the resurrection call of their sermons! Holiness springs up in their wake as flowers at the voice of spring, and where they tread the desert blooms as the garden of the Lord. God's cause demands such leaders along the whole line of official position from subaltern to superior. How feeble, aimless, or worldly are our efforts, how demoralised and vain for God's work without them!

The gift of these leaders is not in the range of ecclesiastical power. They are God's gifts. Their being, their presence, their number, and their ability are the tokens of His favour; their lack the sure sign of His disfavour, the presage of His withdrawal. Let the Church of God be on her knees before the Lord of hosts, that He may more mightily endow the leaders we already have, and put others in rank, and lead all along the line of our embattled front.

The world is coming into the Church at many points and in many ways. It oozes in; it pours in; it comes in with brazen front or soft, insinuating disguise; it comes in at the top and comes in at the bottom; and percolates through many a hidden way.

For praying men and holy men we are looking — men whose presence in the Church will make it like a censer of holiest incense flaming up to God. With God the man counts for everything. Rites, forms, organisations are of small moment; unless they are backed by the holiness of the man they are offensive in His sight. "Incense is an abomination unto Me; the new moons and sabbaths, the calling of assemblies I cannot away with; it is iniquity, even the solemn meeting."

Why does God speak so strongly against His own ordinances? Personal purity had failed. The impure man tainted all the sacred institutions of God and defiled them. God regards the man in so important a way as to put a kind of discount on all else. Men have built Him glorious temples and have striven and exhausted themselves to please God by all manner of gifts; but in lofty strains He has rebuked these proud worshippers and rejected their princely gifts.

"Heaven is My throne and the earth is My footstool: where is the house that ye build unto Me? and where is the place of My rest? For all those things hath Mine hand made, and all those things hath been, saith the Lord. He that killeth an ox is as if he slew a man; he that sacrificeth a lamb, as if he cut off a dog's neck; he that offereth an oblation, as if he offered swine's blood; he that burneth incense, as if he blessed an idol." Turning away in disgust from these costly and profane offerings, He declares: "But to this man will I look, even to him that is poor and of a contrite spirit, and trembleth at My word."

This truth that God regards the personal purity of the man is fundamental. This truth suffers when ordinances are made much of and forms of worship multiply. The man and his spiritual character depreciate as Church ceremonials increase. The simplicity of worship is lost in religious aesthetics, or in the gaudiness of religious forms.

This truth that the personal purity of the individual is the only thing God cares for is lost sight of when the Church begins to estimate men for what they have. When the Church eyes a man's money, social standing, his belongings in any way, then spiritual values are at a fearful discount, and the tear of penitence, the heaviness of guilt are never seen at her portals. Worldly bribes have opened and stained its pearly gates by the entrance of the impure.

This truth that God is looking after personal purity is swallowed up when the Church has a greed for numbers. "Not numbers, but personal purity is our aim," said the fathers of Methodism. The parading of

Church statistics is mightily against the grain of spiritual religion. Eyeing numbers greatly hinders the looking after personal purity. The increase of quantity is generally at a loss of quality. Bulk abates preciousness.

The age of Church organisation and Church machinery is not an age noted for elevated and strong personal piety. Machinery looks for engineers and organisations for generals, and not for saints, to run them. The simplist organisation may aid purity as well as strength; but beyond that narrow limit organisation swallows up the individual and is careless of personal purity; push, activity, enthusiasm, zeal for an organisation, come in as the vicious substitutes for spiritual character. Holiness and all the spiritual graces of hardy culture and slow growth are discarded as too slow and too costly for the progress and rush of the age. By dint of machinery, new organisations, and spiritual weakness, results are vainly expected to be secured which can only be secured by faith, prayer, and waiting on God.

The man and his spiritual character is what God is looking after. If men, holy men, can be turned out by the easy process of Church machinery readier and better than by the old-time processes, we would gladly invest in every new and improved patent; but we do not believe it. We adhere to the old way — the way the holy prophets went, the king's highway of holiness.

An example of this is afforded by the case of William Wilberforce. High in social position, a member of Parliament, the friend of Pitt the famous statesman, he was not called of God to forsake his high social position nor to quit Parliament, but he was called to order his life according to the pattern set by Jesus Christ and to give himself to prayer. To read the story of his life is to be impressed with its holiness and its devotion to the claims of the quiet hours alone with God. His conversion was announced to his friends — to Pitt and others — by letter.

In the beginning of his religious career he records: "My chief reasons for a day of secret prayer are, (1) That the state of public affairs is very critical and calls for earnest deprecation of the Divine displeasure. (2) My station in life is a very difficult one, wherein I am at a loss to know how to act. Direction, therefore, should be specially sought from time to time. (3) I have been graciously supported in difficult situations of a public nature. I have gone out and returned home in safety, and found a kind reception has attended me. I would humbly hope, too, that what I am now doing is a proof that God has not withdrawn His Holy Spirit from me. I am covered with mercies."

The recurrence of his birthday led him again to review his situation and employment. "I find," he wrote, "that books alienate my heart from God as much as anything. I have been framing a plan of study for myself, but let me remember but one thing is needful, that if my heart cannot be kept in a spiritual state without so much prayer, meditation, Scripture reading, etc., as are incompatible with study, I must *seek first* the righteousness of God." All were to be surrendered for spiritual advance. "I fear," we find him saying, "that I have not studied the Scriptures enough. Surely in the summer recess I ought to read the Scriptures and hour or two every day, besides prayer, devotional reading and meditation. God will prosper me better if I wait on Him. The experience of all good men shows that without constant prayer and watchfulness the life of God in the soul stagnates. Doddridge's morning and evening devotions were serious matters. Colonel Gardiner always spent hours in prayer in the morning before he went forth. Bonnell practised private devotions largely morning and evening, and repeated Psalms dressing and undressing to raise his mind to heavenly things. "I would look up to God to make the means effectual. I fear that my devotions are too much hurried, that I do not read Scripture enough. I must grow in grace; I must love God more; I must feel the power of Divine things more. Whether I am more or less learned signifies not. Whether even I execute the work which I deem useful is comparatively unimportant. But beware my soul of lukewarmness."

The New Year began with the Holy Communion and new vows. "I will press forward," he wrote, "and labour to know God better and love Him more. Assuredly I may, because God will give His Holy Spirit to them that ask Him, and the Holy Spirit will shed abroad the love of God in the heart. O, then, pray, pray; be earnest, press forward and follow on to know the Lord. Without watchfulness, humiliation and prayer, the sense of Divine things must languish." To prepare for the future he said he found nothing more effectual than private prayer and the serious perusal of the New Testament.

And again: "I must put down that I have lately too little time for private devotions. I can sadly confirm Doddridge's remark that when we go on ill in the closet we commonly do so everywhere else. I must mend here. I am afraid of getting into what Owen calls the trade of sinning and repenting ... Lord help me, the shortening of private devotions starves the soul; it grows lean and faint. This must not be. I must redeem more time. I see how lean in spirit I become without full allowance of time for private devotions; I must be careful to be watching unto prayer."

At another time he puts on record: "I must try what I long ago heard was the rule of E—— the great upholsterer, who, when he came from Bond Street to his little villa, always first retired to his closet. I have been keeping too late hours, and hence have had but a hurried half hour to myself. Surely the experience of all good men confirms the proposition, that without due measure of private devotions, the soul will grow lean.''

To his son he wrote: ''Let me conjure you not to be seduced into neglecting, curtailing or hurrying over your morning prayers. Of all things, guard against neglecting God in the closet. There is nothing more fatal to the life and power of religion. More solitude and earlier hours — prayer three times a day at least. How much better might I serve if I cultivated a closer communication with God.''

Wilberforce knew the secret of a holy life. Is that not where most of us fail? We are so busy with other things, so immersed even in doing good and in carrying on the Lord's work, that we neglect the quiet seasons of prayer with God, and before we are aware of it our soul is lean and impoverished.

''One night alone in prayer,'' says Spurgeon, ''might make us new men, changed from poverty of soul to spiritual wealth, from trembling to triumphing. We have an example of it in the life of Jacob. Aforetime the crafty shuffler, always bargaining and calculating, unlovely in almost every respect, yet one night in prayer turned the supplanter into a prevailing prince, and robed him with celestial grandeur. From that night he lives on the sacred page as one of the nobility of heaven. Could not we, at least now and then, in these weary earthbound years, hedge abot a single night for such enriching traffic with the skies? What, have we no sacred ambition? Are we deaf to the yearnings of Divine love? Yet, my brethren, for wealth and for science men will cheerfully quit their warm couches, and cannot we do it now and again for the love of God, and the good of souls? Whcrc is our zcal, our gratitude, our sincerity? I am ashamed while I thus upbraid both myself and you. May we often tarry at Jabbok, and cry with Jacob, as he grasped the angel —

> 'With thee all night I mean to stay,
> And wrestle till the break of day.'

Surely, brethren, if we have given whole days to folly, we can afford a space for heavenly wisdom. Time was when we gave whole nights to chambering and wantonness, to dancing and the world's revelry; we did not tire then; we were chiding the sun that he rose so soon, and wishing the hours would lag awhile that we might delight in wilder merriment and perhaps deeper sin. Oh, wherefore, should we weary in heavenly employments? Why grow we weary when asked to watch with our Lord? Up sluggish heart, Jesus calls thee! Rise and go forth to meet the Heavenly Friend in the place where He manifests Himself."

We can never expect to grow in the likeness of our Lord unless we follow His example and give more time to communion with the Father. A revival of real praying would produce a spiritual revolution.

IX

Bear up the hands that hang down, by faith and prayer; support the tottering knees. Have you any days of fasting and prayer? Storm the throne of grace and persevere therein, and mercy will come down.
—John Wesley

We must remember that the goal of prayer is the ear of God. Unless that is gained the prayer has utterly failed. The utterings of it may have kindled devotional feeling in our minds, the hearing of it may have comforted and strengthened the hearts of those with whom we have prayed, but if the prayer has not gained the heart of God, it has failed in its essential purpose.

A mere formalist can always pray so as to please himself. What has he to do but to open his book and read the prescribed words, or bow his knee and repeat such phrases as suggest themselves to his memory or his fancy? Like the Tartarian Praying Machine, give but the wind and the wheel, and the business is full arranged. So

75

much knee-bending and talking, and the prayer is done. The formalist's prayers are always good, or, rather, always bad, alike. But the living child of God never offers a prayer which pleases himself; his standard is above his attainments; he wonders that God listens to him, and though he knows he will be heard for Christ's sake, yet he accounts it a wonderful instance of condescending mercy that such poor prayers as his should ever reach the ears of the Lord God of Sabaoth.

—C. H. Spurgeon

It may be said with emphasis that no lazy saint prays. Can there be a lazy saint? Can there be a prayerless saint? Does not slack praying cut short sainthood's crown and kingdom? Can there be a cowardly soldier? Can there be a saintly hypocrite? Can there be virtuous vice? It is only when these possibilities are brought into being that we then can find a prayerless saint.

To go through the motion of praying is a dull business, though not a hard one. To say prayers in a decent, delicate way is not heavy work. But to pray really, to pray till hell feels the ponderous stroke, to pray till the iron gates of difficulty are opened, till the mountains of obstacles are removed, till the mists are exhaled and the clouds are lifted, and the sunshine of a cloudless day brightens — this is hard work, but it is God's work and man's best labour. Never was the toil of hand, head and heart less spent in vain than when praying. It is hard to wait and press and pray, and hear no voice, but stay till God answers. The joy of answered prayer is the joy of a travailing mother when a man child is born in to the world, the joy of a slave whose chains have been burst asunder and to whom new life and liberty have just come.

A bird's-eye view of what has been accomplished by prayer shows what we lost when the dispensation of real prayer was substituted by Pharisaical pretence and sham; it shows, too, how imperative is the need for holy men and women who will give themselves to earnest, Christlike praying.

It is not an easy thing to pray. Back of the praying there must lie all the conditions of prayer. These conditions are possible, but they are not to be seized on in a moment by the prayerless. Present they always may be to the faithful and holy, but cannot exist in nor be met by a frivolous, negligent, laggard spirit. Prayer does not stand alone. It is not an isolated performance. Prayer stands in closet connection with all the duties of an ardent piety. It is the issuance of a character which is made up of the elements of a vigorous and commanding faith. Prayer honours God, acknowledges His being, exalts His power, adores His providence, secures His aid. A sneering half-rationalism cries out against devotion, that it does nothing but pray. But to pray well is to do all things well. If it be true that devotion does nothing but pray, then it does nothing at all. To do nothing but pray fails to do the praying, for the antecedent, coincident, and subsequent conditions of prayer are but the sum of all the energised forces of a practical, working piety.

The possibilities of prayer run parallel with the promises of God. Prayer opens an outlet for the promises, removes the hindrances in the way of their execution, puts them into working order, and secures their gracious ends. More than this, prayer like faith, obtains promises, enlarges their operation, and adds to the measure of their results. God's promises were to Abraham and to his seed, but many a barren womb, and many a minor obstacle stood in the way of the fulfillment of these promises; but prayer removed them all, made a highway for the promises, added to the facility and speediness of their realisation, and by prayer the promise shone bright and perfect in its execution.

The possibilities of prayer are found in its allying itself with the purposes of God, for God's purposes and man's praying are the combination of all potent and omnipotent forces. More than this, the possibilities of prayer are seen in the fact that it changes the purposes of God. It is in the very nature of prayer to plead and give directions. Prayer is not a negation. It is a positive force. It never rebels against the will of God, never comes into conflict with that will, but that it does seek to change God's purpose is evident. Christ said, "The cup which My Father hath given Me shall I not drink it?" and yet He had prayed that very night, "If it be possible let this cup pass from Me." Paul sought to change the purposes of God about the thorn in his flesh. God's purposes were fixed to destroy Israel, and the prayer of Moses changed the purposes of God and saved Israel. In the time of the Judges Israel were apostate and greatly oppressed. They repented and cried unto God and He said: "Ye have forsaken Me and served other gods, wherefore I will deliver you no more:" but they humbled themselves, put away their strange gods, and God's "soul was grieved for the misery of Israel," and he sent them deliverance by Jephthah.

God sent Isaiah to say to Hezekiah, "Set thine house in order: for thou shalt die, and not live." and Hezekiah prayed, and God sent Isaiah back to say, "I have heard thy prayer, I have seen thy tears; behold I will add unto thy days fifteen years." "Yet forty days and Nineveh shall be overthrown," was God's message by Jonah. But Nineveh cried mightily to God, and "God repented of the evil that He had said He would do unto them; and

He did it not."

The possibilities of prayer are seen from the diverse' conditions it reaches and the diverse' ends it secures. Elijah prayed over a dead child, and it came to life; Elisha did the same thing; Christ prayed at Lazarus's grave, and Lazarus came forth. Peter kneeled down and prayed beside dead Dorcas, and she opened her eyes and sat up, and Peter presented her alive to the distressed company. Paul prayed for Publius, and healed him. Jacob's praying changed Esau's murderous hate into the kisses of the tenderest brotherly embrace. God gave to Rebecca Jacob and Esau because Isaac prayed for her. Joseph was the child of Rachel's prayers. Hannah's praying gave Samuel to Israel. John the Baptist was given to Elizabeth, barren and past age as she was, in answer to the prayer of Zacharias. Elisha's praying brought famine or harvest to Israel; as he prayed so it was. Ezra's praying carried the Spirit of God in heart-breaking conviction to the entire city of Jerusalem, and brought them in tears of repentance back to God. Isaiah's praying carried the shadow of the sun back ten degrees on the dial of Ahaz.

In answer to Hezekiah's praying an angel slew one hundred and eighty-five thousand of Sennacherib's army in one night. Daniel's praying opened to him the vision of prophecy, helped him to administer the affairs of a mighty kingdom, and sent an angel to shut the lions' mouths. The angel was sent to Cornelius, and the Gospel opened through him to the Gentile world, because his "prayers and alms had come up as a memorial before God." "And what shall I more say? for the time would fail me to tell of Gideon, and of Barak, and of Samson, and of Jephthah; of David also, and Samuel, and of the prophets;" of Paul and Peter, and John and the Apostles, and the holy company of saints, reformers, and martyrs, who, through praying, "subdued king-doms, wrought righteousness, obtained promises, stop-ped the mouths of lions, quenched the violence of fire, escaped the edge of the sword, out of weakness were made strong, waxed valiant in fight, turned to flight the armies of the aliens."

Prayer puts God in the matter with commanding force: "Ask of Me things to come concerning My sons," says God, "and concerning the work of My hands com-mand ye Me." We are charged in God's Word "always to pray," "in everything by prayer," "continuing inst-ant in prayer," to "pray everywhere," "praying always." The promise is as illimitable as the command is comprehensive. "All things whatsoever ye shall ask in prayer, believing, ye shall receive," "whatever ye shall ask," "if ye shall ask anything." "Ye shall ask what ye will and it shall be done unto you." "Whatsoever ye ask the Father He will give it to you." If there is anything not involved in "All things whatsoever," or not found in the phrase "Ask anything," then these things may be left out of prayer. Language could not cover a wider range, nor involve more fully all *minutia*. These state-ments are but samples of the all-comprehending possi-bilities of prayer under the promises of God to those who meet the conditions of right praying.

These passages, though, give but a general outline of the immense regions over which prayer extends its sway. Beyond these the effects of prayer reach and secure good from regions which cannot be traversed by language or thought. Paul exhausted language and thought in praying, but conscious of necessities not covered and realms of good not reached he covers these impenetrable and undiscovered regions by this general plea, "unto Him that is able to do exceeding abundantly above all that we ask or think, according to the power that worketh in us." The promise is, "Call upon Me, and I will answer thee, and show thee great and mighty things, which thou knowest not."

James declares that "the effectual, fervent prayer of a righteous man availeth much." How much he could not tell, but illustrates it by the power of Old Testament praying to stir up New Testament saints to imitate by the fervour and influence of their praying the holy men of old, and duplicate and surpass the power of their praying. Elijah, he says, was a man subject to like passions as we are, and he prayed earnestly that it might not rain: and it rained not on the earth by the space of three years and six months. And he prayed again, and the heaven gave rain, and the earth brought forth her fruit.

In the Revelation of John the whole lower order of God's creation and His providential government, the Church and the angelic world, are in the attitude of waiting on the efficiency of the prayers of the saintly ones on earth to carry on the various interests of earth and heaven. The angel takes the fire kindled by prayer and casts it earthward, "and there were voices, and thunderings, and lightnings, and an earthquake." Prayer is the force which creates all these alarms, stirs, and throes. "Ask of Me," says God to His Son, and to the Church of His Son, "and I shall give Thee the nations for Thine inheritance and the uttermost parts of the earth for Thine possessions."

The men who have done mighty things for God have always been mighty in prayer, have well understood the possibilities of prayer, and made most of the possibilities. The Son of God, the first of all and the mightiest of all, has shown us the all-potent and far-reaching possibilities of prayer. Paul was might for God because he knew how to use, and how to get others to use, the mighty spiritual forces of prayer.

The seraphim, burning, sleepless, adoring, is the figure of prayer. It is resistless in its ardour, devoted and tireless. There are hindrances to prayer that nothing but pure, intense flame can surmount. There are toils and outlays and endurance which nothing but the strongest, most ardent flame can abide. Prayer may be low-tongued, but it cannot be cold-tongued. Its words may be few, but they must be on fire. Its feelings may not be impetuous, but they must be white with heat. It is the effectual, fervent prayer that influences God.

God's house is the house of prayer; God's work is the work of prayer. It is the zeal for God's house and the zeal for God's work that makes God's house glorious and His work abide.

When the prayer-chambers of saints are closed or are entered casually or coldly, then Church rulers are secular, fleshly, materialised; spiritual character sinks to a low level, and the ministry becomes restrained and enfeebled.

When prayer fails, the world prevails. When prayer fails the Church loses its Divine characteristics, its Divine power; the Church is swallowed up by a proud ecclesiasticism, and the world scoffs at its obvious impotence.

X

I look upon all the four Gospels as thoroughly genuine, for there is in them the reflection of a greatness which emanated from the person of Jesus and which was of as Divine a kind as ever was seen on earth.

—Goethe

There are no possibilities, no necessity for prayerless praying, a heartless performance, a senseless routine, a dead habit, a hasty, careless performance — it justifies nothing. Prayerless praying has no life, gives no life, is dead, breathes out death. Not a battle-axe but a child's toy, for play not for service. Prayerless praying does not come up to the importance and aims of a recreation. Prayerless praying is only a weight, an impediment in the hour of struggle, of intense conflict, a call to retreat in the moment of battle and victory.

Why do we not pray? What are the hindrances to prayer? This is not a curious nor trivial question. It goes not only to the whole matter of our praying, but to the whole matter of our religion. Religion is bound to decline when praying is hindered. That which hinders praying, hinders religion. He who is too busy to pray will be too busy to live a holy life.

Other duties become pressing and absorbing and crowd out prayer. Choked to death, would be the coroner's verdict in many cases of dead praying, if an inquest could be secured on this dire, spiritual calamity. This way of hindering prayer becomes so natural, so easy, so innocent that it comes on us all unawares. If we will allow our praying to be crowded out, it will always be done. Satan had rather we let the grass grow on the path to our prayer-chamber than anything else. A closed chamber of prayer means gone out of business religiously or what is worse, made an assignment and carrying on our religion in some other name than God's and to somebody else's glory. God's glory is only secured in the business of religion by carrying that religion on with a large capital of prayer. The apostles understood this when they declared that their time must not be employed in even the sacred duties of alms-giving; they must give themselves, they said, "continually to prayer and to the ministry of the Word," prayer being put first with them and the ministry of the Word having its efficiency and life from prayer.

The process of hindering prayer by crowding out is simple and goes by advancing stages. First, prayer is hurried through. Unrest and agitation, fatal to all devout exercises, come in. Then the time is shortened, relish for the exercise palls. Then it is crowded into a corner and depends on the fragments of time for its exercise. Its value depreciates. The duty has lots its importance. It no longer commands respect nor brings benefit. It has fallen out of estimate, out of heart, out of the habits, out of the life. We cease to pray and cease to live spiritually.

There is no stay to the desolating floods of worldliness and business and cares, but prayer. Christ meant this when He charged us to watch and pray. There is no pioneering corps for the Gospel but prayer. Paul knew that when he declared that "night and day he prayed exceedingly that we might see your face and might perfect that which is lacking in your faith." There is no arriving at a high state of grace without much praying and no staying in those high altitudes without great praying. Epaphras knew this when he "laboured fervently in prayers" for the Colossian Church, "that they might stand perfect and complete in all the will of God."

The only way to preserve our praying from being hindered is to estimate prayer at its true and great value. Estimate it as Daniel did, who, when he "knew that the writing was signed he went into his house, and his windows being opened to Jerusalem, he kneeled upon his knees three times a day and prayed and gave thanks before his God as he did aforetime." Put praying into the high values as Daniel did, above place, honour, ease, wealth, life. Put praying into the habits as Daniel did. "As he did aforetime," has much in it to give firmness and fidelity in the hour of trial; much in it to remove hindrances and master opposing circumstances.

One of Satan's wiliest tricks is to destroy the best by the good. Business and other duties are good, but we are so filled with these that they crowd out and destroy the best. Prayer holds the citadel for God, and if Satan can by any means weaken prayer he is a gainer so far, and when prayer is dead the citadel is taken. We must keep prayer as the faithful sentinel keeps guard, with sleepless vigilance. We must not keep it half-starved and feeble as a baby, but we must keep it in giant strength. Our prayer-chamber should have our freshest strength, our calmest time, its hours unfettered, without obtrusion, without haste. Private place and plenty of time are the life of prayer. "To kneel upon our knees three times a day and pray and give thanks before God as we did aforetime," is the very heart and soul of religion, and makes men, like Daniel, of "an excellent spirit," "greatly beloved in heaven."

The greatness of prayer, involving as it does the whole man, in the intensest form, is not realised without spiritual discipline. This makes it hard work, and before this exacting and consuming effort our spiritual sloth or feebleness stands abashed.

The simplicity of prayer, its child-like elements form a great obstacle to true praying. Intellect gets in the way of the heart. The child spirit only is the spirit of prayer. It is no holiday occupation to make the man a child again. In song, in poetry, in memory he may wish himself a child again, but in prayer he must be a child again in reality. At his mother's knee, artless, sweet, intense, direct, trustful. With no shade of doubt, no temper to be denied. A desire which burns and consumes which can only be voiced by a cry. It is no easy work to have this child-life spirit of prayer.

If praying were but an hour in the closet, difficulties would face and hinder even that hour, but praying is the whole life preparing for the closet. How difficult it is to cover home and business, all the sweets and all the bitters of life, with the holy atmosphere of the closet! A holy life is the only preparation for prayer. It is just as difficult to pray, as it is to live a holy life. In this we find a wall of exclusion built around our closets; men do not love holy praying, because they do not love and will not do holy living. Montgomery sets forth the difficulties of true praying when he declares the sublimity and simplicity of prayer.

> Prayer is the simplest form of speech
>   That infant lips can try.
> Prayer is the sublimest strains that reach
>   The Majesty on high.

This is not only good poetry, but a profound truth as to the loftiness and simplicity of prayer. There are great difficulties in reaching the exalted, angelic strains of prayer. The difficulty of coming down to the simplicity of infant lips is not much less.

Prayer in the Old Testament is called wrestling. Conflict and skill, strenuous, exhaustive effort are involved. In the New Testament we have the terms striving, labouring fervently, fervent, effectual, agony, all indicating intense effort put forth, difficulties overcome. We, in our praises sing out —

> "What various hindrances we meet
> In coming to a mercy seat."

We also have learned that the gracious results secured by prayer are generally proportioned to the outlay in removing the hindrances which obstruct our soul's high communion with God.

Christ spake a parable to this end, that men ought always to pray and not faint. The parable of the importunate widow teaches the difficulties in praying, how they are to be surmounted, and the happy results which follow from valorous praying. Difficulties will always obstruct the way to the closet as long as it remains true,

"That Satan trembles when he sees
The weakest saint upon his knees."

Courageous faith is made stronger and purer by mastering difficulties. These difficulties but couch the eye of faith to the glorious prize which is to be won by the successful wrestler in prayer. Men must not faint in the contest of prayer, but to this high and holy work they must give themselves, defying the difficulties in the way, and experience more than an angel's happiness in the results. Luther said: "To have prayed well is to have studied well." More than that, to have prayed well is to have fought well. To have prayed well is to have lived well. To pray well is to die well.

Prayer is a rare gift, not a popular, ready gift. Prayer is not the fruit of natural talents; it is the product of faith, of holiness, of deeply spiritual character. Men learn to pray as they learn to love. Perfection in simplicity, in humility in faith — these form its chief ingredients. Novices in these graces are not adepts in prayer. It cannot be seized upon by untrained hands; graduates in heaven's highest school of art can alone touch its finest keys, raise its sweetest, highest notes. Fine material, fine finish are requisite. Master workmen are required, for mere journeymen cannot execute the work of prayer.

The spirit of prayer should rule our spirits and our conduct. The spirit of the prayer-chamber must control our lives or the closet hour will be dull and sapless. Always praying in spirit; always acting in the spirit of praying; these make our praying strong. The spirit of every moment is that which imparts strength to the closet communion. It is what we are out of the closet gives victory or brings defeat to the closet. If the spirit of the world prevails in our non-closet hours, the spirit of the world will prevail in our closet hours, and that will be a vain and idle farce.

We must live for God out of the closet if we would meet God in the closet. We must bless God by praying lives if we would have God's blessing in the closet. We must do God's will in our lives if we would have God's ear in the closet. We must listen to God's voice in public if we would have God listen to our voice in private. God must have our hearts out of the closet, if we would have God's presence in the closet. If we would have God in the closet, God must have us out of the closet. There is no way of praying to God, but by living to God. The closet is not a confessional, simply, but the hour of holy communion and high and sweet intercourse and of intense intercession.

Men would pray better if they lived better. They would get more from God if they lived more obedient and well pleasing to God. We would have more strength and time for the Divine work of intercession if we did not have to expend so much strength and time settling up old scores and paying our delinquent taxes. Our spiritual liabilities are so greatly in excess of our spiritual assets that our closet time is spent in taking out a decree of bankruptcy instead of being the time of great spiritual wealth for us and for others. Our closets are too much like the sign, "Closed for Repairs."

John said of primitive Christian praying, "Whatsoever we ask we receive of Him, because we keep His commandments and do those things which are pleasing in His sight." We should note what illimitable grounds were covered, what illimitable gifts were received by their strong praying: "Whatsoever" — how comprehensive the range and reception of mighty praying; how suggestive the reasons for the ability to pray and to have prayers answered. Obedience, but more than mere obedience, doing the things which please God well. They went to their closets made strong by their strict obedience and loving fidelity to God in their conduct. Their lives were not only true and obedient, but they were thinking about things above obedience, searching for and doing things to make God glad. These can come with eager step and radiant countenance to meet their Father in the closet, not simply to be forgiven, but to be approved and to receive.

It makes much difference whether we come to God as a criminal or a child; to be pardoned or to be approved; to settle scores or to be embraced; for punishment or for favour. Our praying to be strong must be buttressed by holy living. The name of Christ must be honoured by our lives before it will honour our intercessions. The life of faith perfects the prayer of faith.

Our lives not only give colour to our praying, but they give body to it as well. Bad living makes bad praying. We pray feebly because we live feebly. The stream of praying cannot rise higher than the fountain of living. the closet force is made up of the energy which flows from the confluent streams of living. The feebleness of living throws its faintness into closet homes. We cannot talk to God strongly when we have not lived for God strongly. The closet cannot be made holy to God when the life has not been holy to God. The Word of God emphasises our conduct as giving value to our praying. "Then shalt thou call and the Lord shalt answer, Thou shalt cry and He shall say, Here I am. If thou take away from the midst of thee the yoke, the putting forth the finger, and speaking vanity."

Men are to pray "lifting up holy hands without wrath and doubting." We are to pass the time of our sojourning here in fear if we would call on the Father. We cannot divorce praying from conduct. "Whatsoever we ask we receive of Him because we keep His commandments and do those things that are pleasing in His sight." "Ye ask and receive not because ye ask amiss that ye may consume it upon your lusts." the injunction of Christ, "Watch and pray," is to cover and guard conduct that we may come to our closets with all the force secured by a vigilant guard over our lives.

Our religion breaks down oftenest and most sadly in our conduct. Beautiful theories are marred by ugly lives. The most difficult as well as the most impressive point in piety is to live it. Our praying suffers as much as our religion from bad living. Preachers were charged in primitive times to preach by their lives or preach not at all. So Christians everywhere ought to be charged to pray by their lives or pray not at all. Of course, the prayer of repentance is acceptable. But repentance means to quit doing wrong and learn to do well. A repentance which does not produce a change in conduct is a sham. Praying which does not result in pure conduct is a delusion. We have missed the whole office and virtue of praying if it does not rectify conduct. It is in the very nature of things that we must quit praying or quit bad conduct. Cold, dead praying may exist with bad conduct, but cold, dead praying is no praying in God's esteem. Our praying advances in power as it rectifies the life. A life growing in its purity and devotion will be a more prayerful life.

The pity is that so much of our praying is without object or aim. It is without purpose. How much praying there is by men and women who never abide in Christ — hasty praying, sweet praying full of sentiment, pleasing praying, but not backed by a life wedded to Christ. Popular praying! How much of this praying is from unsanctified hearts and unhallowed lips! Prayers spring into life under the influence of some great excitement, by some pressing emergency, through some popular clamour, some great peril. But the conditions of prayer are not there. We rush into God's presence and try to link Him to our cause, inflame Him with our passions, move Him by our peril. All things are to be prayed for — but with clean hands, with absolute deference to God's will and abiding in Christ. Prayerless praying by lips and hearts untrained to prayer, by lives out of harmony with Jesus Christ; prayerless praying, which has the form and motion of prayer but is without the true heart of prayer, never moves God to an answer. It is of such praying that James says: "Ye have not because ye ask not; ye ask and receive not, because ye ask amiss."

The two great evils — not asking, and asking in a wrong way. Perhaps the greater evil is wrong asking, for it has in it the show of duty done, of praying when there has been no praying — a deceit, a fraud, a sham. The times of the most praying are not really the times of the best praying. The Pharisees prayed much, but they were actuated by vanity; their praying was the symbol of their hypocrisy by which they made God's house of prayer a den of robbers. Theirs was praying on state occasions — mechanical, perfunctory, professional, beautiful in words, fragrant in sentiment, well ordered, well received by the ears that heard, but utterly devoid of every element of real prayer.

The conditions of prayer are well ordered and clear — abiding in Christ; in His name. One of the first necessities, if we are to grasp the infinite possibilities of prayer, is to get rid of prayerless praying. It is often beautiful in words and in execution; it has the drapery of prayer in rich and costly form, but it lacks the soul of praying. We fall so easily into the habit of prayerless service, of merely filling a programme.

If men only prayed on all occasions and in every place where they go through the motion! If there were only holy inflamed hearts back of all these beautiful words and gracious forms! If there were always uplifted hearts in these erect men who are uttering flawless but vain words before God! If there were always reverent bended hearts when bended knees are uttering words before God to please men's ears!

There is nothing that will preserve the life of prayer; its vigour, sweetness, obligations, seriousness and value, so much as a deep conviction that prayer is an approach to God, a pleading with God, an asking of God. Reality will then be in it; reverence will then be in the attitude, in the place, and in the air. Faith will draw, kindle and open. Formality and deadness cannot live in this high and all-serious home of the soul.

Prayerless praying lacks the essential element of true praying; it is not based on desire, and is devoid of earnestness and faith. Desire burdens the chariot of prayer, and faith drives its wheels. Prayerless praying has no burden, because no sense of need; no ardency, because none of the vision, strength, or glow of faith. No mighty pressure to prayer, no holding on to God with the deathless, despairing grasp, "I will not let Thee go except Thou bless me." No utter self-abandon, lost in the throes of a desperate, pertinacious, and consuming plea: "Yet now if Thou wilt forgive their sin — if not, blot me, I pray Thee, out of Thy book;" or "Give me Scotland, or I die." Prayerless praying stakes nothing on the issue, for it has nothing to stake. It comes with empty hands, indeed, but they are listless hands as well as empty. They have never learned the lesson of empty hands clinging to the cross; this lesson to them has no form nor comeliness.

Prayerless praying has no heart in its praying. The lack of heart deprives praying of its reality, and makes it an empty and unfit vessel. Heart, soul, life must be in our praying; the heavens must feel the force of our crying, and must be brought into oppressed sympathy for our bitter and needy state. A need that oppresses us, and has no relief but in our crying to God, must voice our praying.

Prayerless praying is insincere. It has no honesty at heart. We name in words what we do not want in heart. Our prayers give formal utterance to the things for which our hearts are not only not hungry, but for which they really have no taste. We once heard an eminent and saintly preacher, now in heaven, come abruptly and sharply on a congregation that had just risen from prayer, with the question and statement, "What did you pray for? If God should take hold of you and shake you, and demand what you prayed for, you could not tell Him to save your life what the prayer was that has just died from your lips." So it always is, prayerless praying has neither memory nor heart. A mere form, a heterogeneous mass, an insipid compound, a mixture thrown together for sound and to fill up, but with neither heart nor aim, is prayerless praying. A dry routine, a dreary drudge, a dull and heavy task is this prayerless praying.

But prayerless praying is much worse than either task or drudge, it divorces praying from living; it utters its words against the world, but with heart and life runs into the world; it prays for humility, but nurtures pride; prays for self-denial, while indulging the flesh. Nothing exceeds in gracious results true praying, but better not to pray at all than to pray prayerless prayers, for they are but sinning, and the worst of sinning is to sin on our knees.

The prayer habit is a good habit, but praying by dint of habit only is a very bad habit. This kind of praying is not conditioned after God's order, nor generated by God's power. It is not only a waste, a perversion, and a delusion, but it is a prolific source of unbelief. Prayer-less praying gets no results. God is not reached, self is not helped. It is better not to pray at all than to secure no results from praying. Better for the one who prays, better for others. Men hear of the prodigious results which are to be secured by prayer: the matchless good promised in God's Word to prayer. These keen-eyed worldlings or timid little faith ones mark the great dis-crepancy between the results promised and results realis-ed, and are led necessarily to doubt the truth and worth of that which is so big in promise and so beggarly in re-sults. Religion and God are dishonoured, doubt and un-belief are strengthened by much asking and no getting.

In contrast with this, what a mighty force prayerful praying is. Real prayer helps God and man. God's King-dom is advanced by it. The greatest good comes to man by it. Prayer can do anything that God can do. The pity is that we do not believe this as we ought, and we do not put it to the test.

XI

The deepest need of the Church today is not for any material or external thing, but the deepest need is spiritual. Prayerless work will never bring in the kingdom. We neglect to pray in the prescribed way. We seldom enter the closet and shut the door for a season of prayer. Kingdom interests are pressing on us thick and fast and we must pray. Prayerless giving will never evangelise the world. —Dr. A. J. Gordon

The great subject of prayer, that comprehensive need of the Christian's life, is intimately bound up in the personal fulness of the Holy Spirit. It is "by the One Spirit we have access unto the Father" (Eph. ii. 18), and by the same Spirit, having entered the audience chamber through the "new and living way," we are enabled to pray in the will of God (Rom. viii. 15, 26-27; Gal. iv. 6; Eph. vi. 18; Jude 20-21).

Here is the secret of prevailing prayer, to pray under a direct inspiration of the Holy Spirit, whose petitions for

*us and through us are always according to the Divine
purpose, and hence certain of answer. "Praying in the
Holy Ghost" is but co-operating with the will of God,
and such prayer is always victorious. How many Christians there are who cannot pray, and who seek by effort,
resolve, joining prayer circles, etc., to cultivate in themselves the "holy art of intercession," and all to no purpose. Here for them and for all is the only secret of a
real prayer life — "Be filled with the Spirit," who is
"the Spirit of grace and supplication."*
                              —Rev. J. Stuart Holden, M.A.

The preceding chapter closed with the statement that
prayer can do anything that God can do. It is a tremendous statement to make, but it is a statement borne out
by history and experience. If we are abiding in Christ —
and if we abide in Him we are living in obedience to His
holy will — and approach God in His name, then there
lie open before us the infinite resources of the Divine
treasurehouse.

The man who truly prays gets from God many things
denied to the prayerless man. The aim of all real praying
is to get the thing prayed for, as the child's cry for bread
has for its end the getting of bread. This view removes
prayer clean out of the sphere of religious perfor-
mances. Prayer is not acting a part or going through
religious motions. Prayer is neither official nor formal
nor ceremonial, but direct, hearty, intense. Prayer is not
religious work which must be gone through, and avails
because well done. Prayer is the helpless and needy child
crying to the compassion of the Father's heart and the
bounty and power of a Father's hand. The answer is as
sure to come as the Father's heart can be touched and
the Father's hand moved.

The object of asking is to receive. The aim of seeking is to find. The purpose of knocking is to arouse attention and get in, and this is Christ's iterated and reiterated asseveration that the prayer without doubt will be answered, its end without doubt secured. Not by some round-about way, but by getting the very thing asked for.

The value of prayer does not lie in the number of prayers, or the length of prayers, but its value is found in the great truth that we are privileged by our relations to God to unburden our desires and make our requests known to God, and He will relieve by granting our petitions. The child asks because the parent is in the habit of granting the child's requests. As the children of God we need something and we need it badly, and we go to God for it. Neither the Bible nor the child of God knows anything of that half-infidel declaration, that we are to answer our own prayers. God answers prayer. The true Christian does not pray to stir himself up, but his prayer is the stirring up of himself to take hold of God. The heart of faith knows nothing of that specious scepticism which stays the steps of prayer and chills its ardour by whispering that prayer does not affect God.

D. L. Moody used to tell a story of a little child whose father and mother had died, and who was taken into another family. The first night she asked whether she could pray as she used to do. They said: "Oh, yes!" So she knelt down and prayed as her mother had taught her; and when that was ended, she added a little prayer of her own: "O God, make these people as kind to me as father and mother were." Then she paused and looked up, as if expecting the answer, and then added: "Of course you will." How sweetly simple was that little one's faith! She expected God to answer and "do," and "of course" she got her request, and that is the spirit in which God invites us to approach Him.

In contrast to that incident is the story told of the quaint Yorkshire class leader, Daniel Quorm, who was visiting a friend. One forenoon he came to the friend and said, "I am sorry you have met with such a great disappointment."

"Why, no," said the man, "I have not met with any disappointment."

"Yes," said Daniel, "you were expecting something remarkable today."

"What do you mean?" said the friend.

"Why you prayed that you might be kept sweet and gentle all day long. And, by the way things have been going, I see you have been greatly disappointed."

"Oh," said the man, "I thought you meant something particular."

Prayer is mighty in its operations, and God never disappoints those who put their trust and confidence in Him. They may have to wait long for the answer, and they may not live to see it, but the prayer of faith never misses its object.

"A friend of mine in Cincinnati had preached his sermon and sank back in his chair, when he felt impelled to make another appeal," says Dr. J. Wilbur Chapman. "A boy at the back of the church lifted his hand. My friend left the pulpit and went down to him, and said, 'Tell me about yourself.' The boy said, 'I live in New York. I am a prodigal. I have disgraced my father's name and broken my mother's heart. I ran away and told them I would never come back until I became a Christian or they brought me home dead.' That night there went from Cincinnati a letter telling his father and mother that their boy had turned to God.

"Seven days later, in a black-bordered envelope, a reply came which read: 'My dear boy, when I got the news that you had received Jesus Christ the sky was overcast; your father was dead.' Then the letter went on to tell how the father had prayed for his prodigal boy with his last breath, and concluded, 'You are a Christian tonight because your old father would not let you go.'"

A fourteen-year-old boy was given a task by his father. It so happened that a group of boys came along just then and wiled the boy away with them, and so the work went undone. But the father came home that evening and said, "Frank, did you do the work that I gave you?" "Yes, sir," said Frank. He told an untruth, and his father knew it, but said nothing. It troubled the boy, but he went to bed as usual. Next morning his mother said to him, "Your father did not sleep all last night."

"Why didn't he sleep?" asked Frank.

His mother said, "He spent the whole night praying for you."

This sent the arrow into his heart. He was deeply convicted of his sin, and knew no rest until he had got right with God. Long afterward, when the boy became Bishop Warne, he said that his decision for Christ came from his father's prayer that night. He saw his father keeping his lonely and sorrowful vigil praying for his boy, and it broke his heart. Said he, "I can never be sufficiently grateful to him for that prayer."

An evangelist, much used of God, has put on record that he commenced a series of meetings in a little church of about twenty members who were very cold and dead, and much divided. A little prayer-meeting was kept up by two or three women. "I preached, and closed at eight o'clock," he says. "There was no one to speak or pray. The next evening one man spoke.

"The next morning I rode six miles to a minister's study, and kneeled in prayer. I went back, and said to the little church:

"'If you can make out enough to board me, I will stay until God opens the windows of heaven. God has promised to bless these means, and I believe He will.'

"Within ten days there were so many anxious souls that I met one hundred and fifty of them at a time in an inquiry meeting, while Christians were praying in another house of worship. Several hundred, I think, were converted. It is safe to believe God."

A mother asked the late John B. Gough to visit her son to win him to Christ. Gough found the young man's mind full of sceptical notions, and impervious to argument. Finally, the young man was asked to pray, just once, for light. He replied: "I do not know anything perfect to whom or to which I could pray." "How about your mother's love?" said the orator. "Isn't that perfect? Hasn't she always stood by you, and been ready to take you in, and care for you, when even your father had really kicked you out?" The young man choked with emotion, and said, "Y-e-s, sir; that is so." "Then pray to Love — it will help you. Will you promise?" He promised. That night the young man prayed in the privacy of his room. He kneeled down, closed his eyes, and struggling a moment uttered the words: "O Love." Instantly as by a flash of lightning, the old Bible text came to him: "God is love," and he said, brokenly, "O God!" Then another flash of Divine truth, and a voice said, "God so loved the world, that He gave His only begotten Son," — and there, instantly, he exclaimed, "O Christ, Thou incarnation of Divinest love, show me light and truth." It was all over. He was in the light of the most perfect peace. He ran downstairs, adds the narrator of this incident, and told his mother that he was saved. That young man is today an eloquent minister of Jesus Christ.

A water famine was threatened in Hakodate, Japan. Miss Dickerson, of the Methodist Episcopal Girls' School, saw the water supply growing less daily, and in one of the fall months appealed to the Board in New York for help. There was no money on hand, and nothing was done. Miss Dickerson inquired the cost of putting down an artesian well, but found the expense too great to be undertaken. On the evening of December 31st, when the water was almost exhausted, the teachers and the older pupils met to pray for water, though they had no idea how their prayer was to be answered. A couple of days later a letter was received in the New York office which ran something like this: "Philadelphia, January 1st. It is six o'clock in the morning of New Year's Day. All the other members of the family are asleep, but I was awakened with a strange impression that some one, somewhere, is in need of money which the Lord wants me to supply." Enclosed was a cheque for an amount which just covered the cost of the artesian well and the piping of the water into the school buildings.

"I have seen God's hand stretched out to heal among the heathen in as mighty wonder-working power as in apostolic times," once said a well-known minister to the writer. "I was preaching to two thousand famine orphaned girls, at Kedgaum, India, at Ramabai's Mukti (salvation) Mission. A swarm of serpents as venomous and deadly as the reptile that smote Paul, suddenly raided the walled grounds, 'sent of Satan,' Ramabai said, and several of her most beautiful and faithful Christian girls were smitten by them, two of them bitten twice. I saw four of the very flower of her flock in convulsions at once, unconscious and apparently in the agonies of death.

"Ramabai believes the Bible with an implicit and obedient faith. There were three of us missionaries there. She said: 'We will do just what the Bible says, I want you to minister for their healing according to James v. 14-18.' She led the way into the dormitory where her girls were lying in spasms, and we laid our hands upon their heads and prayed, and anointed them with oil in the name of the Lord. Each of them was healed as soon as anointed and sat up and sang with faces shining. That miracle and marvel among the heathen mightily confirmed the word of the Lord, and was a profound and overpowering proclamation of God."

Some years ago, the record of a wonderful work of grace in connection with one of the stations of the China Inland Mission attracted a good deal of attention. Both the number and spiritual character of the converts had been far greater than at other stations where the consecration of the missionaries had been just as great at the more fruitful place.

This rich harvest of souls remained a mystery until Hudson Taylor on a visit to England discovered the secret. At the close of one of his addresses a gentleman came forward to make his acquaintance. In the conversation which followed, Mr. Taylor was surprised at the accurate knowledge the man possessed concerning this inland China station. "But how is it," Mr. Taylor asked, "that you are so conversant with the conditions of that work?" "Oh!" he replied, "the missionary there and I are old college-mates; for years we have regularly corresponded; he has sent me names of enquirers and converts, and these I have daily taken to God in prayer."

At last the secret was found! A praying man at home, praying definitely, praying daily, for specific cases among the heathen. That is the real intercessory missionary.

Hudson Taylor himself, as all the world knows, was a man who knew how to pray and whose praying was blessed with fruitful answers. In the story of his life, told by Dr. and Mrs. Howard Taylor, we find page after page aglow with answered prayer. On his way out to China for the first time, in 1853, when he was only twenty-one years of age, he had a definite answer to prayer that was a great encouragement to his faith. "They had just come through the Dampier Strait, but were not yet out of sight of the islands. Usually a breeze would spring up after sunset and last until about dawn. The utmost use was made of it, but during the day they lay still with flapping sails, often drifting back and losing a good deal of the advantage gained at night." The story continues in Hudson Taylor's own words:

"This happened notably on one occasion when we were in dangerous proximity to the north of New Guinea. Saturday night had brought us to a point some thirty miles off the land, and during the Sunday morning service, which was held on deck, I could not fail to see that the Captain looked troubled and frequently went over to the side of the ship. When the service was ended I learnt from him the cause. A four-knot current was carrying us toward some sunken reefs, and we were already so near that it seemed improbable that we should get through the afternoon in safety. After dinner, the long boat was put out and all hands endeavored, without success, to turn the ship's head from the shore.

"After standing together on the deck for some time in silence, the Captain said to me:

"'Well, we have done everything that can be done. We can only await the result.'

"A thought occurred to me, and I replied: 'No, there is one thing we have not done yet.'

"'What is that?' he queried.

"'Four of us on board are Christians. Let us each retire to his own cabin, and in agreed prayer ask the Lord to give us immediately a breeze. He can as easily send it now as at sunset.'

"The Captain complied with this proposal. I went and spoke to the other two men, and after prayer with the carpenter, we all four retired to wait upon God. I had a good but very brief season in prayer, and then felt so satisfied that our request was granted that I could not continue asking, and very soon went up again on deck. The first officer, a godless man, was in charge. I went over and asked him to let down the clews or corners of the mainsail, which had been drawn up in order to lessen the useless flapping of the sail against the rigging.

"'What would be the good of that?' he answered roughly.

"I told him we had been asking a wind from God; that it was coming immediately; and we were so near the reef by this time that there was not a minute to lose.

"With an oath and a look of contempt, he said he would rather see a wind than hear of it.

"But while he was speaking I watched his eye, following it up to the royal, and there, sure enough, the corner of the topmost sail was beginning to tremble in the breeze.

"'Don't you see the wind is coming? Look at the royal!' I exclaimed.

"'No, it is only a cat's paw,' he rejoined (a mere puff of wind).

"'Cat's paw or not,' I cried, 'pray let down the mainsail and give us the benefit.'

"This he was not slow to do. In another minute the heavy tread of the men on deck brought up the Captain from his cabin to see what was the matter. The breeze had indeed come! In a few minutes we were ploughing our way at six or seven knots an hour through the water ... and though the wind was sometimes unsteady, we did not altogether lose it until after passing the Pelew Islands.

"Thus God encouraged me," adds this praying saint, "ere landing on China's shores to bring every variety of need to Him in prayer, and to expect that He would honour the name of the Lord Jesus and give the help each emergency required."

In an address at Cambridge some time ago (reported in "The Life of Faith," April 3rd, 1912), Mr. S. D. Gordon told in his own inimitable way the story of a man in his own country, to illustrate from real life the fact of the reality of prayer, and that it is not mere talking.

"This man," said Mr. Gordon, "came of an old New England family, a bit farther back an English family. He was a giant in size, and a keen man mentally, and a university-trained man. He had gone out West to live, and represented a prominent district in our House of Congress, answering to your House of Commons. He was a prominent leader there. He was reared in a Christian family, but he was a sceptic, and used to lecture against Christianity. He told me he was fond, in his lectures, of proving, as he thought, conclusively, that there was no God. That was the type of his infidelity.

"One day he told me he was sitting in the Lower House of Congress. It was at the time of a Presidential Election, and when party feeling ran high. One would have thought that was the last place where a man would be likely to think about spiritual things. He said: 'I was sitting in my seat in that crowded House and that heated atmosphere, when a feeling came to me that the God, whose existence I thought I could successfully disprove, was just there above me, looking down on me, and that He was displeased with me, and with the way I was doing. I said to myself, "This is ridiculous, I guess I've been working too hard. I'll go and get a good meal and take a long walk and shake myself, and see if that will take this feeling away."' He got his extra meal, took a walk, and came back to his seat, but the impression would not be shaken off that God was there and was displeased with him. He went for a walk, day after day, but could never shake the feeling off. Then he went back to his constituency in his State, he said, to arrange matters there. He had the ambition to be the Governor of his State, and his party was the dominant party in the State, and, as far as such things could be judged, he was in the line to become Governor there, in one of the most dominant States our our Central West. He said: 'I went home to fix that thing up as far as I could, and to get ready for it. But I had hardly reached home and exchanged greetings, when my wife, who was an earnest Christian woman, said to me that a few of them had made a little covenant of prayer that I might become a Christian.' He did not want her to know the experience that he had just been going through, and so he said as carelessly as he could, 'When did this thing begin, this praying of yours?' She named the date. Then he did some very quick thinking, and he knew, as he thought back, that it was the day on the calendar when that strange impression came to him for the first time.

"He said to me: 'I was tremendously shaken. I wanted to be honest. I was perfectly honest in not believing in God, and I thought I was right. But if what she said was true, then merely as a lawyer sifting his evidence in a case, it would be good evidence that there was really something in their prayer. I was terrifically shaken, and wanted to be honest, and did not know what to do. That same night I went to a little Methodist chapel, and if somebody had known how to talk with me, I think I should have accepted Christ that night.' Then he said that the next night he went back again to that chapel, where meetings were being held each night, and there he kneeled at the altar, and yielded his great strong will to the will of God. Then he said, 'I knew I was to preach,' and he is preaching still in a Western State. That is half of the story. I also talked with his wife — I wanted to put the two halves together, so as to get the bit of teaching in it all — and she told me this. She had been a Christian — what you call a nominal Christian — a strange confusion of terms. Then there came a time when she was led into a full surrender of her life to the Lord Jesus Christ. Then she said, 'At once there came a great intensifying of desire that my husband might be a Christian, and we made that little compact to pray for him each day until he became a Christian. That night I was kneeling at my bedside before going to rest, praying for my husband, praying very earnestly and then a voice said to me, "Are you willing for the results that will come if your husband is converted?"' The little message was so very distinct that she said she was frightened; she had never had such an experience. But she went on praying still more earnestly, and again there came the quiet voice, 'Are you willing for the consequences?' And again there was a sense of being startled, frightened. But she still went on praying, and wondering what this meant, and a third time the quiet voice came more quietly than ever as she described it, 'Are you willing for the consequences?'

"Then she told me she said with great earnestness, 'O God, I am willing for anything Thou dost think good, if only my husband may know Thee, and become a true Christian man.' She said that instantly, when that prayer came from her lips, there came into her heart a wonderful sense of peace, a great peace that she could not explain, a 'peace that passeth understanding,' and from that moment — it was the very night of the covenant, the night when her husband had that first strange experience — the assurance never left her that he would accept Christ. But all those weeks she prayed with the firm assurance that the result was coming. What were the consequences? They were of a kind that I think no one would think small. She was the wife of a man in a very prominent political position; she was the wife of a man who was in the line of becoming the first official of his State, and she officially the first lady socially of that State, with all the honour that that social standing would imply. Now she is the wife of a Methodist preacher, with her home changed every two or three years, she going from this place to that, a very differemt social position, and having a very different income that she would otherwise have had. Yet I never met a woman who had more of the wonderful peace of God in her heart and of the light of God in her face, that that woman.''

And Mr. Gordon's comment on that incident is this: ''Now, you can see at once that there was no change in the purpose of God through that prayer. The prayer worked out His purpose; it did not change it. But the woman's surrender gave the opportunity of working out the will that God wanted to work out. If we might give ourselves to Him and learn His will, and use all our strength in learning His will and bending to His will, then we would begin to pray, and there is simply nothing that could resist the tremendous power of the prayer. Oh for more men who will be simple enough to get in touch with God, and give Him the mastery of the whole life, and learn His will, and then give themselves, as Jesus gave Himself, to the sacred service of intercession!''

To the man or woman who is acquainted with God and who knows how to pray, there is nothing remarkable in the answers that come. They are sure of being heard, since they ask in accordance with what they know to be the mind and the will of God. Dr. William Burt, Bishop of Europe in the Methodist Episcopal Church, tells that a few years ago, when he visited their Boys' School in Vienna, he found that although the year was not up, all available funds had been spent. He hesitated to make a special appeal to his friends in America. He counselled with the teachers. They took the matter to God in earnest and continued prayer, believing that He would grant their request. Ten days later Bishop Burt was in Rome, and there came to him a letter from a friend in New York, which read substantially thus: "As I went to my office on Broadway one morning (and the date was the very one on which the teachers were praying), a voice seemed to tell me that you were in need of funds for the Boys' School in Vienna. I very gladly enclose a cheque for the work.'' The cheque was for the amount needed. There had been no human communication between Vienna and New York. But while they were yet speaking God answered them.

Some time ago there appeared in an English religious weekly the report of an incident narrated by a well-known preacher in the course of an address to children. For the truth of the story he was able to vouch. A child lay sick in a country cottage, and her younger sister heard the doctor say, as he left the house, "Nothing but a miracle can save her.'' The little girl went to her money-box, took out the few coins it contained, and in perfect simplicity of heart went to shop after shop in the village street, asking, "Please, I want to buy a miracle.''

From each she came away disappointed. Even the local chemist had to say, "My dear, we don't sell miracles here." But outside his door two men were talking, and had overheard the child's request. One was a great doctor from a London hospital, and he asked her to explain what she wanted. When he understood the need, he hurried with her to the cottage, examined the sick girl and said to the mother: "It is true — only a miracle can save her, and it must be performed at once." He got his instruments, performed the operation, and the patient's life was saved.

D. L. Moody gives this illustration of the power of prayer: "While in Edinburgh, a man was pointed out to me by a friend, who said: 'That man is chairman of the Edinburgh Infidel Club.' I went and sat beside him and said, 'My friend, I am glad to see you in our meeting. Are you concerned about your welfare?'

"'I do not believe in any hereafter.'

"'Well, just get down on your knees and let me pray for you.'

"'No, I do not believe in prayer.'

"I knelt beside him as he sat, and prayed. He made a great deal of sport of it. A year after I met him again. I took him by the hand and said: 'Hasn't God answered my prayer yet?'

"'There is no God. If you believe in one who answers prayers, try your hand on me.'

"'Well, a great many are now praying for you, and God's time will come, and I believe you will be saved yet.'

"Some time afterwards I got a letter from a leading barrister in Edinburgh telling me that my infidel friend had come to Christ, and that seventeen of his club men had followed his example.

"I did not know *how* God would answer prayer, but

I knew He would answer. Let us come boldly to God."

Robert Louis Stevenson tells a vivid story of a storm at sea. The passengers below were greatly alarmed, as the waves dashed over the vessel. At last one of them, against orders, crept to the deck, and came to the pilot, who was lashed to the wheel which he was turning without flinching. The pilot caught sight of the terror-stricken man, and gave him a reassuring smile. Below went the passenger, and comforted the others by saying, "I have seen the face of the pilot, and he smiled. All is well."

That is how we feel when through the gateway of prayer we find our way into the Father's presence. We see His face, and we know that all is well, since His hand is on the helm of events, and "even the winds and the waves obey Him." When we live in fellowship with Him, we come with confidence into His presence, asking in the full confidence of receiving and meeting with the justification of our faith.

XII

Let your hearts be much set on revivals of religion. Never forget that the churches have hitherto existed and prospered by revivals; and that if they are to exist and prosper in time to come, it must be by the same cause which has from the first been their glory and defence.—Joel Hawes

If any minister can be satisfied without conversions, he shall have no conversions.—C. H. Spurgeon

I do not believe that my desires for a revival were ever half so strong as they ought to be; nor do I see how a minister can help being in a "constant fever" when his Master is dishonoured and souls are destroyed in so many ways.—Edward Payson

An aged saint once came to the pastor at night and said: "We are about to have a revival." He was asked why he knew so. His answer was, "I went into the

stable to take care of my cattle two hours ago, and there the Lord has kept me in prayer until just now. And I feel that we are going to be revived." It was the commencement of a revival.—H. C. Fish

It has been said that the history of revivals is the history of religion, and no one can study their history without being impressed with their mighty influence upon the destiny of the race. To look back over the progress of the Divine Kingdom upon earth is to review revival periods which have come like refreshing showers upon dry and thirsty ground, making the desert to blossom as the rose, and bringing new eras of spiritual life and activity just when the Church had fallen under the influence of the apathy of the times, and needed to be aroused to a new sense of her duty and responsibility. "From one point of view, and that not the least important," writes Principal Lindsay, in "The Church and the Ministry in the Early Centuries," "the history of the Church flows on from one time of revival to another, and whether we take the awakenings in the old Catholic, the mediaeval, or the modern Church, these have always been the work of men specially gifted with the power of seeing and declaring the secrets of the deepest Christian life, and the effect of their work has always been proportionate to the spiritual receptivity of the generation they have spoken to."

As God, from the beginning, has wrought prominently through revivals, there can be no denial of the fact that revivals are a part of the Divine plan. The Kingdom of our Lord has been advanced in large measure by special seasons of gracious and rapid accomplishment of the work of conversion, and it may be inferred, therefore, that the means through which God has worked in other times will be employed in our time to produce similar results. "The quiet conversion of one sinner after another, under the ordinary ministry of the Gospel," says one writer on the subject, "must always be regarded with feelings of satisfaction and gratitude by the ministers and disciples of Christ; but a periodical manifestation of the simultaneous conversion of thousands is also to be desired, because of its adaptation to afford a visible and impressive demonstration that God has made that same Jesus, Who was rejected and crucified, both Lord and Christ; and that, in virtue of His Divine Mediatorship, He has assumed the royal sceptre of universal supremacy, and 'must reign till all His enemies be made His footstool.' It is, therefore, reasonable to expect that, from time to time, He will repeat that which on the day of Pentecost formed the conclusive and crowning evidence of His Messiahship and Sovereignty; and, by so doing, startle the slumbering souls of careless worldlings, gain the attentive ear of the unconverted, and, in a remarkable way, break in upon those brilliant dreams of earthly glory, grandeur, wealth, power and happiness, which the rebellious and God-forgetting multitude so fondly cherish. Such an outpouring of the Holy Spirit forms at once a demonstrative proof of the completeness and acceptance of His once offering of Himself as a sacrifice for sin, and a prophetic 'earnest' of the certainty that He 'shall appear the second time without sin unto salvation,' to judge the world in righteousness."

And that revivals are to be expected, proceeding, as they do, from the right use of the appropriate means, is a fact which needs not a little emphasis in these days, when the material is exalted at the expense of the spiritual, and when ethical standards are supposed to be supreme. That a revival is not a miracle was powerfully taught by Charles G. Finney. There might, he said, be a miracle among its antecedent causes, or there might not. The Apostles employed miracles simply as a means by which they arrested attention to their message, and established its Divine authority. "But the miracle was not the revival. The miracle was one thing; the revival that followed it was quite another thing. The revivals in the Apostles' days were connected with miracles, but they were not miracles." All revivals are dependent upon God, but in revivals, as in other things, He invites and requires the assistance of man, and the full result is obtained when there is co-operation between the Divine and the human. In other words, to employ a familiar phrase, God alone can save the world, but God cannot save the world alone. God and man unite for the task, the response of the Divine being invariably in proportion to the desire and the effort of the human.

This co-operation, then, being necessary, what is the duty which we, as co-workers with God, require to undertake? First of all, and most important of all — the point which we desire particularly to emphasise — we must give ourselves to prayer. "Revivals," as Dr. J. Wilbur Chapman reminds us, "are born in prayer. When Wesley prayed England was revived; when Knox prayed, Scotland was refreshed; when the Sunday School teachers of Tannybrook prayed, 11,000 young people were added to the Church in a year. Whole nights of prayer have always been succeeded by whole days of soul-winning."

When D. L. Moody's Church in Chicago lay in ashes, he went over to England, in 1872, not to preach, but to listen to others preach while his new church was being built. One Sunday morning he was prevailed upon to preach in a London pulpit. But somehow the spiritual atmosphere was lacking. He confessed afterwards that he never had such a hard time preaching in his life. Everything was perfectly dead, and, as he vainly tried to preach, he said to himself, "What a fool I was to consent to preach! I came here to listen, and here I am preaching." Then the awful thought came to him that he had to preach again at night, and only the fact that he had given the promise to do so kept him faithful to the engagement. But when Mr. Moody entered the pulpit at night, and faced the crowded congregation, he was conscious of a new atmosphere. "The powers of an unseen world seemed to have fallen upon the audience." As he drew towards the close of his sermon he became emboldened to give out an invitation, and as he concluded he said, "If there is a man or woman here who will tonight accept Jesus Christ, please stand up." At once about 500 people rose to their feet. Thinking that there must be some mistake, he asked the people to be seated, and then, in order that there might be no possible misunderstanding, he repeated the invitation, couching it in even more definite and difficult terms. Again the same number rose. Still thinking that something must be wrong, Mr. Moody, for the second time, asked the standing men an women to be seated, and then he invited all who really meant to accept Christ to pass into the vestry. Fully 500 people did as requested, and that was the beginning of a revival in that church and neighbourhood, which brought Mr. Moody back from Dublin, a few days later, that he might assist the wonderful work of God.

The sequel, however, must be given, or our purpose in relating the incident will be defeated. When Mr. Moody preached at the morning service there was a woman in the congregation who had an invalid sister. On her return home she told the invalid that the preacher had been a Mr. Moody from Chicago, and on hearing this she turned pale. "What," she said, "Mr. Moody from Chicago! I read about him some time ago in an American paper, and I have been praying God to send him to London, and to our church. If I had known he was going to preach this morning I would have eaten no breakfast. I would have spent the whole time in prayer. Now, sister, go out of the room, lock the door, send me no dinner; no matter who comes, don't let them see me. I am going to spend the whole afternoon in prayer." And so while Mr. Moody stood in the pulpit that had been like an ice-chamber in the morning, the bedridden saint was holding him up before God, and God, who ever delights to answer prayer, poured out His Spirit in mighty power.

The God of revivals who answered the prayer of His child for Mr. Moody, is willing to hear and to answer the faithful, believing prayers of His people today. Wherever God's conditions are met there the revival is sure to fall. Professor Thos. Nicholson, of Cornell College, U.S.A., relates an experience on his first circuit that impresses anew the old lesson of the place of prayer in the work of God.

There had not been a revival on that circuit in years, and things were not spiritually hopeful. During more than four weeks the pastor had preached faithfully, visited from house to house, in stores, shops, and out-of-the-way places, and had done everything he could. The fifth Monday night saw *many of the official members at lodges,* but only a corporal's guard at the church.

From that meeting the pastor went home, cast down, but not in despair. He resolved to spend that night in prayer. "Locking the door, he took Bible and hymn book and began to inquire more diligently of the Lord, though the meetings had been the subject of hours of earnest prayer. Only God knows the anxiety and the faithful, prayerful study of that night. Near the dawn a great peace and a full assurance came that God would surely bless the plan which had been decided upon, and a text was chosen which he felt sure was of the Lord. Dropping upon the bed, the pastor slept about two hours, then rose, hastily breakfasted, and went nine miles to the far side of the circuit to visit some sick people. All day the assurance increased.

"Toward night a pouring rain set in, the roads were heavy and we reached home, wet, supperless, and a little late, only to find no fire in the church, the lights unlit, and no signs of service. The janitor had concluded that the rain would prevent the service. We changed the order, rang the bell, and prepared for war. Three young men formed the congregation, but in that 'full assurance' the pastor delivered the message which had been prayed out on the preceding night, as earnestly and as fully as if the house had been crowded, then made a personal appeal to each young man in turn. Two yielded, and testified before the meeting closed.

"The tired pastor went to a sweet rest, and next morning, rising a little later than usual, learned that one of the young men was going from store to store throughout the town telling of his wonderful deliverance, and exhorting the people to salvation. Night after night conversions occurred, until in two weeks we heard 144 peole testify in forty-five minutes. All three points of that circuit saw a blaze of revival that winter, and family after family came into the church, until the membership was more than trebled.

"Out of that meeting one convert is a successful pastor in the Michigan Conference, another is the wife of one of the choicest of our pastors, and a third was in the ministry for a number of years, and then went to another denomination, where he is faithful unto this day. Probably none of the members ever knew of the pastor's night of prayer, but he verily believes that God somehow does for the man who thus prays, what He does not do for the man who does not pray, and he is certain that 'more things are wrought by prayer than this world dreams of.'"

All the true revivals have been born in prayer. When God's people become so concerned about the state of religion that they lie on their faces day and night in earnest supplication, the blessing will be sure to fall.

It is the same all down the ages. Every revival of which we have any record has been bathed in prayer. Take, for example, the wonderful revival in Shotts (Scotland) in 1630. The fact that several of the then persecuted ministers would take a part in solemn convocation having become generally known, a vast concourse of godly persons assembled on this occasion from all quarters of the country, and *several days were spent in social prayer,* preparatory to the service. In the evening, instead of retiring to rest, the multitude divided themselves into little bands and *spent the whole night in supplication and praise.* The Monday was consecrated to thanksgiving, a practice not then common, and proved the great days of the feast. After much entreaty, John Livingston, chaplain to the Countess of Wigtown, a young man and not ordained, agreed to preach. He *had spent the night in prayer* and conference — but as the hour of assembling approached his heart quailed at the thought of addressing so many aged and experienced saints, and he actually fled from the duty he had undertaken. But just as the kirk of Shotts was vanishing from his view, those words, "Was I ever a barren wilderness or a land of darkness?" were borne in upon his mind with such force as compelled him to return to the work.

He took for his text Ezekiel xxxvi. 25, 26, and discoursed with great power for about two hours. *Five hundred conversions* were believed to have occurred under that one sermon, thus prefaced by prayer. "It was the sowing of a seed through Clydesdale, so that many of the most eminent Christians of that country could date their conversion, or some remarkable confirmation of their case, from that day."

Of Richard Baxter it has been said that, "he stained his study walls with praying breath; and after becoming thus anointed with the unction of the Holy Ghost he sent a river of living water over Kidderminster." Whitfield once thus prayed, "O Lord, give me souls or take my soul." After much closet pleading, "he once went to the Devil's fair and took more than a thousand souls out of the paw of the lion in a single day."

Mr. Finney says: "I once knew a minister who had a revival fourteen winters in succession. I did not know how to account for it till I saw one of his members get up in a prayer meeting and make a confession. 'Brethren," he said, 'I have been long in the habit of praying every Saturday night till after midnight for the descent of the Holy Ghost among us. And now, brethren (and he began to weep), I confess that I have neglected it for two or three weeks.' The secret was out. That minister had a praying church."

And so we might go on multiplying illustration upon illustration to show the place of prayer in revival and to demonstrate that every mighty movement of the Spirit of God had its source in the prayer-chamber. The lesson of it all is this, that as workers together with God we must regard ourselves as in not a little measure responsible for the conditions which prevail around us today. Are we concerned about the coldness of the Church? Do we grieve over the lack of conversions? Does our soul go out to God in midnight cries for the outpouring of His Spirit?

If not, part of the blame lies at our door. If we do our part, God will do His. Around us is a world lost in sin, above us is a God willing and able to save; it is ours to build the bridge that links heaven and earth, and prayer is the mighty instrument that does the work.

And so the old cry comes to us with insistent voice, "Pray, brethren, pray."

XIII

Lord Jesus, cause me to know in my daily experience the glory and sweetness of Thy name, and then teach me how to use it in my prayer, so that I may be even like Israel, a prince prevailing with God. Thy name is my passport, and secures me access; Thy name is my plea, and secures me answer; Thy name is my honour and secures me glory. Blessed Name, Thou art honey in my mouth, music in my ear, heaven in my heart, and all in all to my being!—C. H. Spurgeon

I do not mean that every prayer we offer is answered exactly as we desire it to be. Were this the case, it would mean that we would be dictating to God, and prayer would degenerate into a mere system of begging. Just as an earthly father knows what is best for his children's welfare, so does God take into consideration the particular needs of His human family, and meets them out of His wonderful storehouse. If our petitions are in accordance with His will, and if we seek His glory

*in the asking, the answers will come in ways that will
astonish us and fill our hearts with songs of thanksgiving. God is a rich and bountiful Father, and He does
not forget His children, nor withhold from them anything which it would be to their advantage to receive.*
—J. Kennedy Maclean

The example of our Lord in the matter of prayer is
one which His followers might well copy. Christ prayed
much and He taught much about prayer. His life and
His works, as well as His teaching, are illustrations of
the nature and necessity of prayer. He lived and
laboured to answer prayer. But the necessity of importunity in prayer was the emphasised point in His
teaching about prayer. He taught not only that men
must pray, but that they must persevere in prayer.

He taught in command and precept the idea of energy
and earnestness in praying. He gives to our efforts
graduation and climax. We are to ask, but to the asking
we must add seeking, and seeking must pass into the full
force of effort in knocking. The pleading soul must be
aroused to effort by God's silence. Denial, instead of
abating or abashing, must arouse its latent energies and
kindle anew its highest ardor.

In the Sermon on the Mount, in which He lays down
the cardinal duties of His religion, He not only gives
prominence to prayer in general and secret prayer in
particular, but He sets apart a distinct and different sec-
tion to give weight to importunate prayer. To prevent
any discouragement in praying He lays as a basic principle the fact of God's great fatherly willingness — that
God's willingness to answer our prayers exceeds our
willingness to give good and necessary things to our children, just as far as God's ability, goodness and perfec-

tion exceed our infirmities and evil. As a further assurance and stimulant to prayer Christ gives the most positive and iterated assurance of answer to prayers. He declares: "Ask and it shall be given to you; seek and ye shall find; knock and it shall be opened unto you." And to make assurance doubly sure, He adds: "For every one that asketh, receiveth; and he that seeketh, findeth; and to him that knocketh it shall be opened."

Why does He unfold to us the Father's loving readiness to answer the prayers of His children? Why does He asseverate so strongly that prayer will be answered? Why does He repeat that positive asseveration six times? Why does Christ on two distinct occasions go over the same strong promises, iterations, and reiterations in regard to the certainty of prayer being answered? Because He knew that there would be delay in many an answer which would call for importunate pressing, and that if our faith did not have the strongest assurance of God's willingness to answer, delay would break it down. And that our spiritual sloth would come in, under the guise of submission, and say it is not God's will to give what we ask, and so cease praying and lose our case. After Christ had put God's willingness to answer prayer in a very clear and strong light, He then urges to importunity, and that every unanswered prayer, instead of abating our pressure should only increase intensity and energy. If asking does not get, let asking pass into the settled attitude and spirit of seeking. If seeking does not secure the answer, let seeking pass on to the more energetic and clamorous plea of knocking. We must persevere till we get it. No failure here if our faith does not break down.

As our great example in prayer, our Lord puts love as a primary condition — a love that has purified the heart from all the elements of hate, revenge, and ill will. Love is the supreme condition of prayer, a life inspired by love. The 13th chapter of 1st Corinthians is the law of prayer as well as the law of love. The law of love is the law of prayer, and to master this chapter from the epistle of St. Paul is to learn the first and fullest condition of prayer.

Christ taught us also to approach the Father in His name. That is our passport. It is in His name that we are to make our petitions known. "Verily, verily, I say unto you, He that believeth on Me, the works that I do shall he do also; and greater *works* than these shall he do; because I go unto the Father. And whatsoever ye shall ask in My name, that will I do, that the Father may be glorified in the Son. If ye shall ask Me anything in My name, that will I do."

How wide and comprehensive is that "whatsoever." There is no limit to the power of that name. "Whatsoever ye shall ask." That is the Divine declaration, and it opens up to every praying child a vista of infinite resource and possibility.

And that is our heritage. All that Christ has may become ours if we obey the conditions. The one secret is prayer. The place of revealing and of equipment, of grace and of power, is the prayer-chamber, and as we meet there with God we shall not only win our triumphs but we shall also grow in the likeness of our Lord and become His living witnesses to men.

Without prayer the Christian life, robbed of its sweetness and its beauty, becomes cold and formal and dead; but rooted in the secret place where God meets and walks and talks with His own, it grows into such a testimony of Divine power that all men will feel its influence and be touched by the warmth of its love. Thus, resembling our Lord and Master, we shall be used for the glory of God and the salvation of our fellow men.

And that, surely is the purpose of all real prayer and the end of all true service.